Collaborative Learning in Practice

Examples from Natural Resource Management in Asia

Edited by

Ronnie Vernooy

International Development Research Centre

Ottawa • Cairo • Dakar • Montevideo • Nairobi • New Delhi • Singapore

FOUNDATION®
BOOKS

Delhi • Bangalore • Mumbai • Kolkata • Chennai • Hyderabad • Pune

Published by
Cambridge University Press India Pvt. Ltd.
Under the Foundation Books imprint
Cambridge House, 4381/4 Ansari Road, Daryaganj, **New Delhi** 110002

Cambridge University Press India Pvt. Ltd.
C-22, C-Block, Brigade M.M., K.R. Road, Jayanagar, **Bangalore** 560 070
Plot No. 80, Service Industries, Shirvane, Sector-1, Nerul, **Navi Mumbai** 400 706
10, Raja Subodh Mullick Square, 2nd Floor, **Kolkata** 700 013
21/1 (New No. 49), 1st Floor, Model School Road, Thousand Lights, **Chennai** 600 006
House No. 3-5-874/6/4, (Near Apollo Hospital), Hyderguda, **Hyderabad** 500 029

Jointly published by Cambridge University Press India Pvt. Ltd. and the International Development Research Centre.

International Development Research Centre
PO Box 8500
Ottawa, ON KIG 3H9
Canada
www.idrc.ca/info@idrc.ca
ISBN (e-book) 978-1-55250-472-7

ISBN 978-81-7596-712-0

Published by Manas Saikia for Cambridge University Press India Pvt. Ltd. and printed at Sanat Printer, Kundli, Haryana.

Contents

Foreword

In 1970, I completed my dissertation with Everett Rogers, the father of Diffusion of Innovations research. At that time, innovation unquestionably seemed to be an "idea perceived as new" that came from outside a community of farmers, doctors, housewives, or other entrepreneurs. It started to affect the community when some of its members adopted the new idea, which eventually led to more-or-less pervasive diffusion.

Economists observed that such change at the individual level has macro effects when new practices begin to affect total supply and start to drive down prices of farm commodities, to sight an example. Then, further, diffusion becomes a matter of surviving in the market place. Such induced innovation came to be understood as an essential aspect of the development "rat race" and the motor of economic growth. All this was no theoretical pie in the sky. Literally, thousands of empirical studies backed this perspective on innovation. At one time, Diffusion of Innovations was the most popular social science research topic ever. Diffusion research diffused with a vengeance.

This understanding of innovation at the level of the firm and its macro economic implications has had, and still has, tremendous impact on practice. Many leading agricultural scientists believe that agricultural development is a question of developing technologies and pushing them out to farmers. Ultimately, agricultural development conveniently is a question of funding scientists. When my 1988 book, *Extension Science: Information Systems in Agricultural Development*, was translated into Chinese, the characters used for extension represented "push" and "shove." We now know that such a limited understanding of innovation and development renders agricultural science unfit for the purpose when it comes to dealing with the challenges we face today. *Collaborative Learning in Practice: Examples from Natural Resource Management in Asia* tackles this issue head on. It provides arguments and evidence for a new approach and gives much needed voice and weight to insights that are emerging across the globe.

In the conventional view, innovation is the emergent property of millions of individuals making rational choices in the market. Notwithstanding the explicit recognition by social scientists, starting with Emile Durkheim, and institutional economists, such as Douglass North, that individual behaviour is embedded in a historical institutional context of negotiated rules of the game, organizational structures, forms of governance, and social capital, to all intents and purpose we still operate on *methodological individualism* – the collective or macro level is seen as an emergent, mechanistic outcome of aggregated individual behaviours.

Today, everything, including that conventional view, is challenged. Although we still call a lack of economic growth "recession," we also know that we have to move beyond growth if we want to deal effectively with an anthropogenic Earth. That is, we can no longer rely on natural processes to ensure fresh water supplies, a stable climate, the regeneration of ecosystems, and other crucial ecosystem services to a biotope, in which billions of humans and other sentient beings can continue to flourish. We also know that economic growth and "trickle down" do not automatically end persistent poverty. In fact, the divide between haves and have-nots only seems to increase. Gone are the days when we could capture, compete, conquer, and corrupt in the certain knowledge that the Earth and "the market" would take care of the externalized costs of our activities. We now know that we have to do that ourselves. That is what we mean by "anthropogenic." We have to deal with the collective impact of human action and its major cause – human behaviour and the institutions in which it is embedded.

We have no idea how to create a society that can handle an anthropogenic Earth. All we know is that our current global economic system of unending growth is incompatible with the drivers that make the troposphere, that flimsy layer of mellowness that envelops the Earth, so conducive to higher life forms. We also know for a fact that the Earth cannot supply the resources required to provide all people to with the lifestyles to which the middle classes in post-industrial countries and elites in emerging countries have become accustomed to. This American lifestyle is not negotiable. Meanwhile, it is threatened by an inadequate food system, a run-away banking crisis, a disproportionate ecological footprint, and unsupportable energy costs, and is sustainable only as long as other countries are willing to foot the bill. Since we all aspire to that kind of life, it is a predicament we all face today. Realizing this has fundamental implications for our understanding of innovation, and thus for any capacity development effort that aims to encourage it.

Innovation is no longer a new *idea* that comes from outside. It is the *process* of transforming our modern society and the ideas that got us where we are. "Business-as-usual is not an option" was the conclusion of the International Assessment of Agricultural Science and Technology for Development that was accepted by 58 governments in

April 2008. Innovation is no longer only a necessary condition for *firms* to survive in the market place, it is now a condition for preserving and regenerating *global society*. For the time being, we have no idea how to go about it. Science can help, but by emphasising cause – effect relations and technical solutions and generally ignoring human institutions as key ingredients of any change in the anthropogenic domain, science has remained part of the problem. It is now increasingly recognized that, in complex contexts, cause-and-effect relations are understandable only in retrospect. Complex contexts, therefore, call for experimental probing and evolutionary approaches that pay attention to the institutional embeddeness of innovation.

The complex context is determined by an interplay of many factors and actors that are not amenable to conventional analysis, prediction, and logical frameworks. New approaches are required to address social learning, multistakeholder processes, innovation systems, and institutional transformation. These approaches are in the stage of exploration, trial-and-error, and uncertainty. Donors are still wary of financing them because of the inherent impossibility of specifying milestones, let alone measurable output, beforehand. Yet there is great urgency to learn about these approaches to institutional development. The future depends on a steep societal learning curve in that respect.

Therefore this book, is very welcome. It was written from the new understanding of innovation, and funded by a donor who did not shrink from open-ended outcomes and deliberately unspecified logical frameworks. It reports the outcome of action-research projects that took to heart the message that "business as usual is not an option." They deliberately experimented and probed new approaches to multistakeholder learning processes as an avenue to institutional change. They describe not only what was done, but also what the understanding was that determined why it was done. They sought new language to communicate about complexity and how we can deal with it. They deliberately sought to scale up their results through curriculum development and policy change.

In all, this book is a welcome effort to develop new scientific approaches to complexity. It is a report of a credible multi-year, cross-disciplinary, and cross-national effort. It fits squarely into the new understanding of innovation that many of us now try to operationalize. I hope it will contribute to a much wider understanding of what is at stake. After all, without a widespread new "literacy" that effectively replaces technology supply push and market fundamentalism, all we can expect is more of the same. When I say this, I speak as someone who has been a life-long student of innovation and is awed by the enormity of managing an anthropogenic Earth. The greatest challenge, as usual, is not to learn new things, but to unlearn old ones and to change existing institutions. The action research reported in this book tackles that issue head on. Go and multiply!

Niels Röling
Emeritus Professor
Communication and Innovation Studies
Wageningen University, The Netherlands
Andelst, 2009

Acknowledgements

Many people came together in the three collaborative learning processes highlighted in this book and, in one way or another, they all contributed to the learning that unfolded. As authors and contributors to this book, we thank all our co-learners for their interest, enthusiasm, and dedication. They illustrate the lesson that effective learning can only take place if we commit and engage fully, with open hearts and open minds.

The team from the International Potato Centre's (also known by its Spanish name, Centro Internacional de la Papa or CIP) Users' Perspectives With Agricultural Research and Development network (UPWARD) thanks all the participating organizations, mentors, resource people, and facilitators in the Participatory Research and Development Programme, especially Liz Fajber, Shantanu Mathur, Alessandro Meschinelli, Gelia Castillo, Tara Lama, Rabi Chitrakar, Mayette Nadal, and Hydee de Chavez.

The reflections and syntheses of experiences and insights presented in the Adaptive Learning and Linkages in Community-Based Natural Resource Management (ALL in CBNRM) case study draw on the collective work and reflections of mentors and colleagues in both the Isang Bagsak and ALL in CBNRM programmes. The ALL in CBNRM team wishes to thank deeply Guy Bessette, Chin Saik Yoon, and Julian Gonsalves as well as colleagues at the University of the Philippines at Los Baños: Professor Emeritus Nora C. Quebral, Lourdes Margarita A. Caballero, Cleofe S. Torres, Luningning A. Matulac, Ma. Theresa H. Velasco, Ma. Stella C. Tirol, Madeline M. Suva, Ines Vivian D. Domingo, Emmanuel Rodantes G. Abraham, Benjamina Paula G. Flor, Serlie B. Jamias, Leah P. Arboleda, Sherwin Joseph C. Felicidario, Aldo Gavril T. Lim, Hermilea Marie P. Cabral, Mildred O. Moscoso, Ma. Teresita B. Osalla, Joclarisse E. Albia, and Mara Katrina Escurel.

The team also wishes to acknowledge the following people in participating organizations – Elmer M. Ferrer, Randee Cabaces, Allan Vera, Tata dela Cruz, Dindo M. Campilan, Arma Bertuso, Carlos S. Basilio, Jaime A. Gallentes, Robert W. Solar, Emily Monville Oro, Jitendra Kumar Sinha, Marion Tan, Marissa B. Espineli, Ronnakorn Triraganon, Noelle O'Brien, Peter John Stephen, Michael Newman, Duncan McLeod, Dao Mong Uyen, Pham Tran Thuy Anh; and the Vietnamese, Indonesia, Philippine, Cambodian, Lao PDR, and Thailand learning groups. The team also expresses thanks to its African Isang Bagsak counterparts led by Jones Kaumba, Christopher Kamlongera,

Claude Adandedjan, and Wilberforce Tushemereirwe. And they thank Ronnie Vernooy, Qi Gubo, Zhang Li, and Dindo Campilan for their comments and shared learning while we worked on the case study and this book.

The China team expresses its gratitude to all the partners who, since 2004, have joined the efforts to mainstream participatory approaches to teaching, training, research, and development work. The "family" includes university students (current and graduates) and staff at the China Agricultural University, Jilin Agricultural University, Hebei Agricultural University, Yunnan University, Guangxi University, the Guizhou University of Finance and Economics, and Shandong Agricultural University; staff and students of the Guizhou Academy of Agricultural Sciences, the Center for Chinese Agricultural Policy, the non-governmental organizations HOPE, and Action-Aid; and farmers, extension agents, and other government staff in Ningxia, Guizhou, Jilin, Yunnan, Guangxi, and Hebei. This family continues to grow.

All three teams appreciate the hospitality provided by the International Development Research Centre's Singapore office, where the first writing workshop leading to this book took place. Elaine Tang, in particular, deserves special thanks. Sandra Garland, once more, improved our English writing. Bill Carman at IDRC and his co-publishing colleagues assured a smooth publication process. We thank our families and close friends for their patience and support.

Ronnie Vernooy

Preface

Recently, capacity development has once again become popular. In a world of struggling, failing, and collapsing institutions and organizations this does not come as a surprise. But capacity development is a complex issue – easier talked about and written about than put into practice.

Webster's Online Dictionary (consulted 29 September, 2008), gives eight definitions of capacity. Among them, are the *ability to perform or produce* and the *power to learn or retain knowledge*. These two definitions seem closely linked when the concept of capacity is applied to a professional field, such as teaching, research, or development planning and implementation. In these fields, professionals are preoccupied with both individual and organizational (what could be called *collective*) learning and performance. Capacity development then refers to strengthening individual and collective abilities to perform one or more tasks or to produce valuable outcomes and impacts.

This book is about collaborative learning for participatory rural development with a focus on community-based natural resource management approaches. Although informed and inspired by capacity development and learning theory, the emphasis of the three in-depth, Asian case studies highlighted here is on rural development practice. The three cases have the following features in common – they focus on *real-life, complex learning situations* concerning natural resource management dilemmas; they are examples of the gradual making of novel *communities of practice* for capacity development; they demonstrate both the process and outcome merits of using *a variety of learning methods;* and they make facilitators an *integral part* of the learning process.

The three cases suggest that effective capacity development is a dynamic, evolving, and unfolding process rather than a linear, mechanistic, or predictable chain of events. The cases demonstrate that the effectiveness of capacity development strategies can be increased through solid grounding in the local context, defining do-able and practice focused learning objectives, integration of expertise, organizational collaboration, deliberate application of utilization-focused participatory monitoring and evaluation, and dynamic process management.

Although the cases cover one particular professional field and are context specific, the insights gained from critical examination of the practices used here provide valuable guidance for other initiatives. Hopefully, more effective capacity development can contribute to more relevant rural development practices and to fewer individual and organizational struggles, failures, and breakdowns.

Ronnie Vernooy
Ottawa, 2010

Coordination and collaboration: performance at the farmer festival
(Kaizuo township, Guiyang province, China).
Photo: Ronnie Vernooy.

1

Toward Centres of Excellence for CBNRM (Community-Based Natural Resource Management)

Ronnie Vernooy and Guy Bessette, with Dindo Campilan and Kevin Kelpin

Mastering action through collaborative learning

"The PR & D [Participatory Research and Development] programme ... at the Assam Agricultural University gave the researchers the opportunity to understand the importance of involving the community in variety selection for upland Ahu rice. More importantly, researchers were exposed to the cultural diversity of different communities ... [and learn more about] their farming practices and livelihood options. They were able to interact with the community on a continuous basis, understand their behavior and rationale for some of the community decisions in rejecting technology improvement in upland Ahu rice."

Sharma and Pathak (2006)

"Before we joined the ALL [Adaptive Learning Linkages] in CBNRM [Community Based Natural Resource Management] programme, frankly, every strategy that we implemented was by trial and error. We did not really have a systematic way of learning. But in this programme, every goal is identified, step by step. Before the mentoring visit, we did not have a specific task for our radio programming. We broadcast every issue to the community. Now, we focus on three main issues: environment, policy, and public service delivery. With this, Yascita [an NGO], can get more information and data that can be used for advocacy."

Muh. Aswan Zanynu, Yascita, Indonesia, 2008 (ALL in CBNRM 2008: 8)

"As someone said, 'You can learn more from the process if you take part in the [CBNRM] course more actively.' I attended the curriculum development planning workshop in January 2006 and, later, during the course, I served as a course assistant. This course is really novel for students. It is interesting and open. The thing that impresses me most is the power of the team. If you trade an apple for someone else's apple, each of you still has only one apple; if you exchange an idea with another, both of you have two ideas. The formulation of the field research plan, the report, the proposal, the short movie (of the field-visit), all taught me many new things. It is really learning by doing. And the course persists in emphasizing the practice. It is very useful for us."

Yang Huan, M.Sc. student, College of Humanities and Development, China Agricultural University, Beijing, April 2006 (Vernooy et al. 2008: 191)

This book is about new ways to design collaborative learning and novel learning results. As the quotations above suggest, learning is about acquiring new knowledge, attitudes, and skills and putting these *into practice.* In the three cases highlighted in this book, the practice of doing participatory, community-based field research contributes to improving rural livelihoods in a sustainable manner.

All the above quotes reveal an instrumentalist perspective on learning – the acquiring of new knowledge and the mastering of certain (professional) skills. Without instrumental knowledge, we would have a hard time coping with challenges in our professional and everyday lives. Knowledge and skills related to instrumental forms of learning can be technical – aimed at analysing, manipulating and "controlling" our environment. They can also be communicative – a means to understand oneself and others through exchange and interpretation (Habermas 1985). Interacting closely and continuously with classmates, teachers, and farmers and critically reflecting on this experience can greatly improve our communicative capacities.

However, the speakers also suggest a broader and deeper learning perspective that includes reflection, the development of a new way of seeing and reasoning, and the exploration of new forms of doing – learning in terms of personal and, sometimes, collective identity development as well. This is not only learning about ourselves and our place in the world by acquiring communicative knowledge, but also developing the capacity to be more reflective about ourselves, i.e., willing and able to question our assumptions, behaviour, modes of learning, and the "construction" of our environment. These dimensions of learning are perhaps more fuzzy, but no less important.

Transformative learning is a deeper type of learning. It implies capacity to see ourselves and our reality in a more holistic manner and act accordingly. As such, transformative learning is integral to praxis – the term used by Freire to describe theory-informed practice (Freire 2000; Mezirow and associates 2000; Percy 2005; Cranton 2006). Several of the participants' experiences – both individual and collective – in the three case studies described in this book are examples of this kind of learning. None of these cases was explicitly designed to achieve this outcome; this learning simply occurred as a result of the activities. Personal identity development is embedded in the acquisition of social learning and adaptive management skills, which are of value beyond people's professional lives (for a more in-depth analysis, see Zhang Li 2008).

It is hard to imagine how one learns alone. Even for mere observation, we depend mostly on others to show us the way. Learning, especially active learning, is an interactive process. We learn by interacting with others, with the help of artefact, and by doing things together with others (Wenger 1998; Wenger et al. 2002; Cranton 2006). In this sense, learning and its outcomes are fundamentally, socially constructed processes (Leeuwis 2002). Learning purposefully and effectively – what we might call the *art of learning* – is very useful.

The three cases in this book tell us that most effective learning takes place by doing things based on a relationship or relationships with others. Therefore, developing meaningful and useful relationships, is another useful capacity, and seemingly central to learning. Certainly, in the case of rural development and natural resource management, characterized increasingly by complex and often conflicting social configurations, this kind of learning, including the capacity to deal with differences, tensions and conflicts, is crucial, although too often neglected.

One of the key lessons derived from the three cases is that *organizational* change processes for addressing natural resource management challenges need to mirror the key elements of successful Community-Based Natural Resource Management (CBNRM) practices, i.e., social learning and adaptive management. Social learning means that various stakeholders learn together and from each other and, collectively, work at addressing complex CBNRM issues. Adaptive management emphasizes the action-reflection-action cycle to enable stakeholders, as social learners, to apply their new learning and improve their actions. When these principles are applied deliberately and continuously, organizational capacity development takes place, not as an end result, but as part of the effort. From what we have learned so far, this indicates the need to pay much more attention to the meso-level, i.e., the formation of new and the strengthening of existing social configurations of like-minded people, within and across organizations.

Dynamic and holistic learning experiences usually encompass an appropriate mix of all three forms of learning, allowing us to get things done, interact with others and with artefacts, adapt to new circumstances, be critical, creative and innovative, develop more fully, and create new links with others. The cases in this book are based on the hypothesis that deliberately created innovative and experimental *collaborative* learning experiences so that it could contribute to more effective learning outcomes and, thus, lead to more effective rural development practice. Thus, the three cases represent novel forms of organizational capacity development, through which, in practice, new meaning is given to the concept of organization. Each case includes reflections on this emerging organizational process, from design, through implementation, to monitoring and evaluation and beyond, i.e., a process of making dynamic and holistic learning an integral part of rural development practice.

Three innovative learning case studies in Asia are highlighted, from different contexts, but with a common approach: CBNRM and Participatory Action Research (PAR). The three cases illustrate learning *together* by doing and experimenting, based on a shared vision, a willingness to cross organizational borders, a commitment to carry out tasks jointly, take risks, and share resources, and the deliberate use of participatory monitoring and evaluation from beginning to end. In Wenger's (1998) sense, they can be seen as examples of emerging communities of capacity development practice or, following Freire, development praxis. Based on this experience and reflection, these initiatives are described as movements toward "centres of capacity development excellence" (Bessette and Vernooy 2005; Large 2006).

The CBNRM–PAR subject matter of all three cases leads to the notion of social learning, defined as the process by which multiple social actors with competing claims or interests move toward, and engage in, negotiations and concerted action at multiple scales of interaction (Röling 2002). It is about learning together and learning from each other, toward the development of collective cognition (in Röling's terms, building on others) – "translated" as the capacity to engage in collective action. Social learning can take place formally or informally, in units, departments, associations, committees, non-governmental organizations (NGOs), and networks of various kinds. The establishment and "management" of learning groups and networks focus on facilitating and inspiring human and social development through learning, innovation, and attention to process, including dealing with disputes and existing or emerging conflicts (see Leeuwis and Pyburn 2002; Wals 2007). One of the main lessons from the cases is that for CBNRM-PAR-oriented capacity development efforts to be effective, the learning process itself ought to be designed and guided as a social learning process.

Thanks to increased mobility and modern communication technologies, people around the world are developing and experimenting with new forms of learning together and learning from each other. The three cases also speak to this new dimension of learning and show how these new technologies can be used to facilitate learning across time and sometimes large distances. However, although web-based tools prove to be very useful, the cases make a strong point that face-to-face interactions remain crucial.

The three cases

Although connected by the common threads discussed above, the cases differ in terms of the people and organizations involved, political and socio-economic situation, local history of "theories" and particular learning practices, and in terms of the scope, timing, and spacing of the initiatives. In this sense, they become true case studies of novel ways of collaborative learning (Yin 2008), allowing comparison and assessment.

The first case is the PR & D programme for South Asia. This programme aimed to strengthen, through a collaborative effort, the capacity of selected individuals and organizations to carry out PR & D in agriculture and natural resource management. The programme focused on regional training and implementation, the identification and assessment of appropriate mechanisms for institutionalizing and scaling up PR & D, and the sharing of lessons learned with those in other developing regions. It used a variety of learning methods with an emphasis on face-to-face interactions, peer review, mentoring, and fieldwork.

Sixteen organizations from five countries in South Asia took part in the programme, including local and international NGOs, universities, and national and international research centres. Collectively, they cover a wide range of subjects – crop production, bio-diversity, forest conservation, health, nutrition, and community development. Coordination was in the hands of two Nepalese NGOs – Nepal Participatory Action Network (NEPAN) and Local Initiatives for Biodiversity, Research and Development (LI-BIRD). The Centro Internacional de la Papa's Asian network, Users' Perspectives With Agricultural Research and Development (CIP-UPWARD), provided technical expertise.

The second case is the Adaptive Learning and Linkages in Community-Based Natural Resource Management (ALL in CBNRM) network for Southeast Asia. ALL in CBNRM aims to create a community of participatory-oriented natural resource management researchers and practitioners and, through networking, a regional CBNRM centre of excellence. The network brings together people from government, NGOs, universities, research organizations, and community-based organizations.

Five organizations coordinate the network – the College of Development Communication at the University of the Philippines in Los Baños, the Regional Community Forestry Training Center for Asia and the Pacific based in Bangkok, the International Institute of Rural Reconstruction in the Philippines, CIP-UPWARD based in the Philippines, and the CBNRM Learning Center in the Philippines. The programme makes use of both interpersonal and web-based learning methods.

The third case brings us to China and the country's higher education system. This initiative – Participatory Learning, Curriculum Development and Mainstreaming of CBNRM approaches in Higher Education in China – aims to contribute to the development and implementation of innovative, community-based and participatory rural development approaches in rural China. The capacity development portion of the intiative, led by working groups at China Agricultural University (CAU) and Jilin Agricultural University (JLAU), has six interrelated components:

1. At the core, participatory curriculum development experiments aimed at introducing CBNRM at the postgraduate level.
2. Supporting CBNRM research by students and staff, to link CBNRM theory with practice and to allow participants to reflect on doing

action research in rural areas and use the results of the field research as inputs for further course development and refinement. This component is implemented through small-grant support for CBNRM thesis fieldwork, supervision of CBNRM students by CAU and JLAU staff jointly with partners, a seminar series for students and interested staff (including those outside CAU and JLAU), and a publication series.

3. Identification and support of "champions" – young, promising students and staff who show initiative and leadership.
4. Sharing of experiences, results, and lessons through teacher–teacher and student–student exchanges and guidance (similar to a farmer-to-farmer approach).
5. Creation of an enabling environment, i.e., longer-term financial and political support from Chinese sources, such as CAU and JLAU leaders, the Ministry of Education, the Ministry of Agriculture, and perhaps complementary funding from donor agencies.
6. Sound and ongoing monitoring. This implies the reinforcement of monitoring and evaluation skills through targeted training and practice and the development and implementation of sound assessment plans.

Structure of the book

These cases are closely examined in the following chapters:

1. Describing how the initiatives are developed – the background and rationale, ideas, and theory of action – and what are the expectations in terms of learning results. Identifying for whom and when the capacities are aimed to be developed.
2. Describing and reflecting critically on what has been done and are in process and the methods used, making use of an ethnographic approach.
3. Highlighting the use of participatory monitoring and evaluation as a means to strengthen the learning processes and outcomes.
4. Synthesizing the changes this learning is thought to have brought about (intended and unintended results) at the individual and organizational levels (specifying in each case what the organizational level encompasses) and trying to answer key questions like: Is changing individual attitudes, knowledge, and

skills contributing to improved CBNRM practices? Are capacity development efforts contributing to more equal and learning-oriented relationships? Is changing individual capacities and learning relationships contributing to the strengthening of organizational performance? Have capacity development efforts contributed to desired CBNRM outcomes, in terms of improved livelihoods, more equal access to natural resources, sustainable use of natural resources, empowerment, and supportive policy changes?

5. Also trying to identify emergent, unplanned elements resulting from the efforts. Some important insights have been obtained.
6. Summarizing and comparing the three cases and the main learning outcomes. Attempting to provide explanations for the results and identifying factors that may be key in terms of design, implementation, and sustainability, i.e., the continuation of learning in time and space, by ourselves and others. Where the understanding of the cases increase, hypothesizing about what would have happened if the initiatives had not been realized. The strengths and weaknesses of the various capacity development designs and strategies and how the wider context (i.e., societal forces) influences outcomes given a particular design are examined.

Key capacities for CBNRM

"I am so excited since I came back from Baicheng [field-visit site in eastern Jilin province]. It is worth doing this kind of research, and this is my first, but most important, thing to experience. I got a lot of information about rural development by visiting the field and reinforcing what I learned in class. The visit not only allowed us to grasp some basic principles of participatory research and development, but also to experience the reality. The participatory method is new for us. It makes our way of learning and doing research more varied and interesting. We now have another way to solve problems. I cherish this choice and feel lucky to have taken part in the course. In this course, everyone can practice his or her ability. We all have the same opportunity, and everyone is eager to participate. To do the work, everyone must work together, just like a harmonious family in which every member plays an important role. This is the spirit of teamwork."

M.Sc. student, JLAU, Changchun, May 2006 (Vernooy et al. 2008: 199)

Natural resource management and rural development problems are complex, diverse and in constant flux. Experiences from across Asia (and elsewhere) provide strong evidence of this. Various researchers argue that dynamic and novel learning processes and methods are required to analyse these problems, carry out interventions and assess alternatives. (Leeuwis and Pyburn 2002; Van den Bor et al. 2000; Vernooy et al. 2005; Tyler 2006; Wals 2007; Armitage et al. 2007). The challenge, then, is to design and carry out research and capacity development that provide both a better understanding of the complexities of social life and a sounder base for action.

At the heart of such an approach is an effort to engage social actors and together with other interested parties:

1. Set research priorities and identify key problems, issues, and opportunities.
2. Analyse the causes that underlie these problems and issues.
3. Take action to find both short– and long-term solutions to the identified. problems or take advantage of opportunities.
4. Learn from these actions and make changes as needed.

Today natural resource management invariably questions situations in which various social actors operate, interact, and often debate and compete over resources, interests, and points of view. Many of the problems arising because of competing interests for these resources require some sort of collective action to be solved (or even addressed). Experience suggests that collective action is more effective when informed by social learning (Tyler 2006; Vernooy et al. 2005, 2008).

The following capacities were identified which are to be developed or strengthened among rural development professionals who have an interest in such natural resource management questions, paying special attention to fostering collective action at both individual and organizational levels (see Morgan 2006 for a useful, discussion of the concept of capacity):

1. The ability to work and learn together with community members and other stakeholders, with a focus on the attitudes, knowledge, and skills needed to decide how to facilitate the planning, implementation, and assessment of CBNRM–PAR, Research and Development (R & D) initiatives.

2. Knowledge, attitudes, and skills necessary to use PAR practically – in stakeholder analysis, consultation and planning, experimentation, and monitoring and evaluation.
3. The ability to express clear views about PAR, link these views with field practices, and communicate effectively about the development outcomes and impacts.
4. The ability to identify locally appropriate, effective individual and organizational capacity-building strategies.
5. The ability to apply a participatory curriculum development approach to reform current teaching programmes and related research activities.
6. Knowledge and skills to manage PAR, teaching, training, and extension for CBNRM–PR & D at the organizational level.

Many researchers and practitioners in the field of natural resource management have a background in biophysics and do not have the social science skills and knowledge needed to work within a participatory research and learning framework. The same can be said about many people involved in decision-making and policy-making. Those working within a PR & D framework quickly realize that there is a strong need to foster multiple and interdisciplinary ways of working. For many social scientists, on the other hand, this means gaining a better understanding of the natural sciences – histories, rationales, research questions, methods. For scientists in all areas, it also requires working together with partners from rural communities, as well as associated social actors or stakeholders, and to speak the same language about PAR and learning, in terms of approaches, tools, and practices.

From individual to organizational capacity development: toward centres of excellence

Organizations doing research in rural development, including the ones highlighted in this book, have been trying to address the issues and challenges outlined above, usually with limited resources and support. Researchers, university staff, trainers, and practitioners (such as extensionists) have called for more effective and more prolonged support. They are searching for clearer and more coherent and dynamic frameworks and tools to enable them to improve their work with rural communities and others in terms of effectiveness, scientific

> "Our research institute had already demonstrated the labour-saving potential of mechanical maize planting, but only on station. We asked ourselves, how will this technology fare in farmers' fields, with farmers using it, and what do they have to say about it? Thus my field research focused on the participatory evaluation of mechanical planting. The Department of Agriculture realized this was helpful in understanding why farmers adopt or reject technologies. My department decided to learn more about how to do PR & D by doing more of it! Our next activity is to apply participatory technology evaluation to tomato varieties."
>
> *M.A.R. Bhuiyan, Department of Agricultural Extension, Bangladesh* (personal communication, *2006)*

quality or rigour, and results. Organizational obstacles and shortcomings – little or no space for innovation, the lack of incentives, little or no recognition from peers – often hamper their work. Policies are often geared to other sectors (high-tech areas, such as biotechnology and information and communication technologies) or are not supportive of novel ways of doing things (although there are exceptions, as illustrated by our case study on mainstreaming CBNRM in China).

The elements, tools and techniques of such innovative frameworks, as well as tools and techniques, already exist, but they are scattered among organizations and countries. Many R & D organizations have experimented with various participatory research and training strategies – participatory monitoring and evaluation (Vernooy et al. 2003), social and gender analysis (Vernooy 2006), participatory development communication (Bessette 2004), use of the sustainable livelihoods framework, etc. However, most of these initiatives have focused on *individual* research capacity building (although some have also addressed team building). How to translate these kinds of efforts into more effective organizational capacity building and longer-term learning processes remains a challenge (see Baser and Morgan [2008] for the results of a capacity-development study based on twenty case studies from around the world).

Knowledge about good practices in building organizational capacity for research in CBNRM is still scarce. A few CBNRM-oriented organizations who are interested face challenges (MacKay et al. 2002; Horton et al. 2003). Institutionalization does not happen as a result of a single research or capacity development project, eloquent policy briefs, or series of publications, but develops through a long-term consistent programme for building capacity and gaining field experience.

Reflecting on this issue, staff at Canada's International Development Research Centre (IDRC) saw an opportunity to bring past and ongoing capacity development efforts and results together to institutionalize CBNRM in national or regional "centres of excellence" – places where future generations of CBNRM scholars, researchers, and practitioners could learn about, practice, improve, and disseminate CBNRM concepts, methods, and achievements. We documented these ideas in a concept paper, presenting what we hoped was a series of clear and coherent ideas that would inspire our own work as well as that of partners (Bessette and Vernooy 2005). Subsequently, when we became more confident of the usefulness of these ideas, we asked an IDRC intern to elaborate on the underlying thoughts more systematically and thoroughly (Large 2006).

"Centres" do not necessarily refer to physical units, such as a university department. A centre could take the form of a network or a community of practice. A community of practice, as described by Wenger (1998), comprises a group of people who share a particular concern or passion for something they are engaged in and who, through *joint activities*, pursue their interest further and learn along the way. The notion of moving *toward* centres of excellence builds on the concept of community of practice, but also highlights the institutional efforts required to ensure the promotion of CBNRM approaches, concepts, methods, and tools. As Wenger points out, this notion of movement toward learning implies regular action based on *cooperation* (mutual engagement) and *commitment to a common agenda.* When action is accompanied by critical reflection – leading to what Freire (2000) called praxis – learning is believed to be more effective. We hypothesized that these three elements – willingness to cooperate, shared goals, and continuous, collective reflection – were key to putting the concept of centres of excellence into practice. The three case studies represent particular ways of giving meaning to the concept.

Increasing the quality of learning: the use of evaluation

> "We are impressed with the Participatory Monitoring and Evaluation (PM & E) strategy used by VECO-Indonesia. We adopted it for our marketing analysis and development for non-timber forest products strategy. Villagers, project officers, and consultants are all involved in indentifying and measuring indicators. The PM & E process helps villagers understand the whole process and realize the stage of marketing development. It also encouraged local people to take more ownership of their actions."
> *Souvanhpheng Phommasane, National Agriculture and Forestry Research Institute, Lao PDR, 2008 (ALL in CBNRM 2008: 9)*

Well-designed, regular monitoring and evaluation can contribute to good practices in CBNRM capacity development (Horton et al. 2003; Vernooy et al. 2003; Engel et al. 2007; Baser and Morgan 2008). A coherent and meaningful evaluative learning framework helps enhance the existing pool of knowledge by offering valuable lessons and insights into effective strategies and factors that lead to success in capacity development. It can also provide a critical view of issues surrounding scaling up, sustainability, and institutionalization. Most R & D organizations routinely monitor and evaluate their capacity development efforts, but mainly in terms of immediate outputs, e.g., changes in knowledge associated with training activities or distribution and readership of publications and knowledge products. This kind of evaluation does not adequately track changes beyond the level of a specific activity.

In the three case studies, the organizations have tried or are trying to go beyond such an approach. They have done so by joining forces with other partners in the region interested in strengthening evaluation expertise for CBNRM capacity development. These efforts have been supported by IDRC through two interlinked activities – an IDRC-wide strategic evaluation of capacity development (Box 1) and a regional project on the evaluation of CBNRM capacity (Box 2).

Box 1. IDRC's strategic evaluation of capacity development

In 2005, IDRC commissioned a strategic evaluation of its capacity development efforts. The study is an attempt to capture how IDRC supports individuals, groups, organizations and networks in their efforts to enhance their capacities in ways that are culturally appropriate, socially relevant and sustainable over time. Overall, the evaluation seeks to elucidate the multiple change processes that both IDRC staff and partners experience as they work toward the enhancement of partners' capacities and the relation between these processes and the outcomes of this work.

Generally, the term "capacity development" represents a process whereby individuals and groups – organizations, networks, communities, institutions, sectors, societies – increase their ability to identify challenges and conduct, manage, and communicate research that addresses these challenges over time and in a sustainable manner.

Equally important is the notion that the capacities of individuals or groups must be understood in relation to the systems in which they are embedded. Individuals apply and develop their capacities within "webs of significance" that they have themselves spun (Geertz 1977) – the organizations, institutions, societies, networks, and general relationships that are meaningful to all human life. Therefore, efforts to facilitate capacity development at one level or in one part of the system will almost always have implications for the others. Recognizing this, the strategic evaluation reflects on the nature and notion of systems and systemic change related to IDRC's capacity development efforts.

The study is composed of several phases: compiling a range of background studies,* exploring IDRC staff's understanding of capacity development and how they have translated this understanding into practical action (Nielson and Lusthaus 2007) and examining a selection of 43 IDRC-supported projects. The latter phase focuses on gathering information through interviews with IDRC partners (who implemented the selected projects) and examining related project documents. The final phase (2007–08) consists of a series of six in-depth case studies to explore the significant issues that emerged from the earlier phases. The cases studies discussed in this book will complement the case studies included in the larger study.

**Source:* IDRC's web site at www.idrc.ca/en/ev-105772-201-1-DO_TOPIC.html.

Box 2. Learning to use evaluation in CBNRM capacity development

In the Asian region, several efforts are being made to document the processes and results of CBNRM-oriented capacity development. However, cross-learning and sharing among organizations in the region have remained limited. This has hindered the identification of good practices, as well as the design of pathways for scaling out and scaling up.

A new initiative started in 2006, which brings together in an informal network, nine Asian partner organizations to develop and pilot methods for evaluating processes and outcomes of capacity development, promote the effective use of evaluation by organizations engaged in capacity development efforts, and facilitate wider learning and use of evaluation in capacity development. Building on the results of previous research concerning organizational development that offers a number of analytical frameworks and methods for assessing capacity and related performance, the project intends to fill a gap in terms of developing approaches that systematically assess both capacity development processes and outcomes. Research will address the following five questions:

1. What are various stakeholders learning from their involvement in capacity development efforts?
2. Are capacity development efforts contributing to more equal and learning-oriented relationships among stakeholders?
3. Have capacity development efforts contributed to desired CBNRM outcomes in terms of improved livelihoods, more equal access to natural resources, sustainable use of natural resources, empowerment and supportive policy changes?
4. What are the strengths and weaknesses of various capacity development modalities, such as, working groups, learning communities, networks and organizational partnerships, for CBNRM outcomes?
5. How should CBNRM capacity development efforts be monitored and evaluated? How can multiple stakeholder perspectives be considered?

These questions are very similar to those addressed in the three case studies in this book. Two of them – "ALL in CBNRM" and "China" case studies – are among those analyzed in the evaluation initiative. The third, the PR & D programme, is no longer active and was not included.

Main points

The three cases in this book are varied examples of innovative practices in terms of collaborative learning for CBNRM. They cover four key areas of capacity development.

First, they include the development of holistic curricula that integrate the various approaches and tools used in the practice of participatory CBNRM and PR & D. The three initiatives offer such curricula (which have in common key concepts, principles and methods, but differ in delivery modalities) to various categories of learners: academics and graduate students, practitioners and researchers in the field, community groups and policymakers. The three cases share the common feature of making curriculum development an *emergent, collective and adapative* production process, instead of a pre-established blueprint delivered by teachers or instructors who know all and who know best.

Second, in each case, knowledge and expertise about CBNRM and PR & D from a diversity of people and organizations is gathered through a prolonged process of working and learning together. This pooling of expertise involves students, researchers, practitioners, community groups, policymakers and staff from international organizations. Although the experience of these social actors varies, they are motivated to join forces and engage in a shared experience, which is actually designed as a learning experiment. Facilitating the sharing of experiences among these participants is a deliberate and continuous effort; although, not without difficulties and tensions.

Third, based on the principle of an action-reflection-sharing-action cycle, collaborative learning can be very effective when it employs participatory action approaches anchored in rural realities. To facilitate learning both at the individual and group or organizational levels, there is a need for a variety of learning methods appropriately blended to maximize advantages and offset weaknesses. These methods include face-to-face discussion, electronic-facilitated discussion, reading of supplementary materials, group discussion with resource people, fieldwork, backstopping and mentoring, provision of and guided production of knowledge resources, small research grants, and workshops. A community of practice can be an effective means to mobilize the expertise required to design and implement appropriate blend of methods, but communities of practice are not established by decree. Organizations must be willing to develop and invest in these new forms of partnerships (Bessette et al. 2008).

Fourth, the cases aim to develop and use effective reflection to increase the quality of the collaborative learning, including the promotion of CBNRM, PR & D, and PAR approaches to key organizational decision-makers and policymakers (i.e., mainstreaming). This is done through the systematic integration of participatory monitoring and evaluation mechanisms from the beginning and throughout the whole process. Advocacy and mainstreaming take place through a variety of means, including policy analysis, peer-to-peer or community-to-community networking, linking communities with other development practitioners and outreach efforts (websites, publications, dissemination events).

Emerging results indicate that partners have strengthened their individual and organizational capacities for CBNRM and PR & D research, training, teaching, extension, advocacy, networking, communication, and dissemination in terms of their knowledge, attitude, skills and practice (including research ethics). They are also strengthening their capacity to manage these functions leading to improved individual and organizational performance, although the latter is more difficult to bring about and requires a clear, coherent, long-term strategy.

The cases show that researchers and practitioners have improved their skills in expressing their views about PR & D, linking them to their practices, communicating more effectively about their work, and, to varying degrees, reflecting critically on their work and their underlying assumptions. The improvement of the skills needed to work effectively is in progress with community members and others to identify relevant problems and solutions and to decide how best to facilitate the planning, experimentation, and assessment of CBNRM-focused R & D initiatives.

Participating local communities are benefiting from the experiences in a number of ways through gradual improvement in their livelihoods, the building or strengthening of social capital (e.g., new or strengthened networks or associations) and, in some cases, stronger policy support. All partners are gaining a better understanding and practical experience with a variety of locally adapted, effective individual and organizational capacity-building strategies allowing them to be more selective while choosing future initiatives and providing better support to them. Although it is difficult to change hierarchical structures, ingrained ways of doing things, and incentive mechanisms that do not favour innovation some policy changes are underway.

Indian farmers collect data on their field trials to assess how new sweet potato varieties perform under local conditions.
Photo: S. Attaluri.

2

Participatory Research and Development in South Asia

Dindo Campilan and Rajindra Ariyabandu with Pratap Shrestha, Raghav Raj Regmi, Carlos Basilio, and Julian Gonsalves

Learning to work with and for local people

> "The PR & D project gave us researchers the opportunity to understand the importance of involving the community in selecting suitable varieties of upland Ahu rice. More important, it helped us better understand the cultural diversity of different farming communities in a similar environment, and learn more about their farming practices and livelihood options. We had the opportunity to interact continuously with the community members, understand their behavior and rationale for some of their decisions for rejecting technology improvement in upland Ahu rice."
>
> *Sharma and Pathak (2006)*

As income and food security have increased for many agricultural communities, the challenge of environmental protection and natural resource management has taken centre stage. Addressing this challenge requires a new approach that involves understanding and sharing of knowledge about livelihood outcomes directly benefiting the poor, enabling the poor to engage in agricultural production while conserving natural resources on a long-term basis, and facilitating joint learning and action within and among local communities. Besides simply transferring technology, the goal of agricultural Research and

Development (R & D) has become more complex and emphasis on sustainable management of natural resources has increased.

A number of R & D organizations around the world have adopted the concept of Participatory Research and Development (PR & D) in an effort to capture the essence of this approach. PR & D was also the focus of a collaborative regional programme for capacity development in South Asia. The following examples (Box 3) illustrate how PR & D capacity development has contributed to improved practice in terms of Community-Based Natural Resource Management (CBNRM).

Box 3. How developing PR & D capacity improves resource management

"In a village in Andhra Pradesh, India, poor and marginalized women formed a self-help group to improve their livelihood by collecting *Pongamia* seeds and extracting their oil, which can be used as fuel with a low rate of carbon emission. Through knowledge gained from on-farm experiments with researchers, the women are now able to sell the oil for 30 rupees a litre (about US $ 0.62). The by-product, which is high in plant nutrients, is used as a fertilizer in crop production. With this innovation, men and women no longer leave the village looking for jobs, not even during the usually lean summer period."

Sreedevi (2006)

"In the high mountains of Bhutan, farming communities learned the importance of collective action in managing irrigation schemes to cope with increased water demand for agricultural use. With guidance from researchers, farmers learned to analyze their irrigation problems and to agree on improved water management schemes. Erosion and gully formation are common problems in hilly terrain irrigation systems in Bhutan. Farmers realized that these problems arose from inappropriate water use practices, and joint recognition of this fact was the starting point for planning and implementing sustainable management of local water."

Dhungyel and Zangmo (2006)

The strength of a PR & D approach is that it works within people's own livelihood frameworks. This has the potential to empower, broaden options, and allow better control of livelihoods. PR & D is also sensitive to users' perspectives and links scientific with local knowledge. For example, in the case described by Sharma and Pathak (at the beginning of this chapter), acceptance criteria of the community were matched with the scientific knowledge of the researchers at Assam Agricultural University to guide the breeding of a new variety that exhibits locally desired traits.

PR & D works in an interdisciplinary mode, seeks to involve multiple stakeholders from related organizations, and strives to be impact driven. In the Andhra Pradesh case, natural resource management scientists were already working with farming households to plant *Pongamia* in local watersheds, as organisms in the roots of these trees fix nitrogen, improving soil quality. The agricultural scientists helped farmers take advantage of the opportunity to use oil from the trees' seeds as fuel for generators and the waste by-product of oil extraction as a fertilizer.

Unlike conventional approaches to research, PR & D demands a set of knowledge, attitudes, and skills beyond those needed for technical research associated with the typical R & D paradigms. Because PR & D requires new ways of thinking about designing and doing research, renewed efforts to develop capacity among researchers and their organizations are necessary (Campilan et al. 2003).

PR & D encompasses a broader set of phases and activities (Gonsalves et al. 2005):

1. *Assessment and diagnosis* – situation analysis, needs and opportunities assessment, problem diagnosis, documentation, and characterization.
2. *Experimenting with technology options* – joint agenda-setting for experimentation, technology development and evaluation, integration of technology components, and piloting.
3. *Sustaining local innovation* – institutionalizing social and political mechanisms, facilitating multiperspective negotiation and conflict management, community mobilization and action, local capacity development, strengthening local partnerships.
4. *Dissemination and scaling up* – development of learning and extension mechanisms, information support to macro-policy development, promoting networking and horizontal linkages.
5. *Managing* – project development, resource mobilization, data management, monitoring and evaluation, PR & D capacity development.

To further promote and develop capacities for PR & D, it is necessary to create more opportunities for information exchange, training, and networking among the growing number of practitioners and organizations seeking to explore the value-added potential of PR & D. Thus, in 2004, three R & D organizations active in South Asia – Local Initiatives for Biodiversity, Research and Development

(LI-BIRD), Nepal Participatory Action Network (NEPAN), and Centro Internacional de la Papa's Asian network, Users' Perspectives With Agricultural Research and Development (CIP-UPWARD) – initiated a programme to renew capacity development among professionals and their organizations in the South Asian region. They believed that the value of PR & D had yet to be fully explored and tapped by the region's wider R & D community. Their main goal was to strengthen researchers' capacities to understand the dynamics of participatory, systems-oriented approaches as a step toward responding more effectively to new rural development challenges (Box 4).

Box 4. Key challenges in PR & D

Capacity development – Developing the PR & D capacity of field practitioners and their organizations, through training, information services, networking and development of protocols.

Establishing support mechanisms for capacity development – Sustaining capacity development through institutionalized, locally driven support mechanisms.

Integration – Creating opportunities and a supportive environment for introducing PR & D into mainstream agriculture and natural resource management programme.

Synthesis – Reviewing diverse PR & D experiences to identify field-tested concepts and practices for wider sharing and adaptation.

The key features of the programme are described in Part 1 of this chapter, including objectives and expected outcomes, partners and participants, strategy and methods, and the use of monitoring and evaluation. The achievements reviewing lessons and challenges, and implications are presented and reflected upon in Part 2.

Part 1: Context, plan, and experiences

The PR & D approach to capacity development: "theory of change"

A PR & D approach uses diverse but interrelated elements to enhance local people's knowledge about sustainable natural resource management. It is based on users' perspectives. Starting with people's own assessment of their situation, it tries to identify opportunities to bring about change. This requires R & D organizations to support and work with local people to share, analyze, and enhance their knowledge of their lives and livelihood conditions and engage them in planning, acting, monitoring, evaluating, and reflecting on new ways of doing things.

In terms of building or strengthening PR & D capacities, this means designing an action agenda that will:

1. Promote understanding of the facilitative nature of a PR & D approach vis-à-vis more technical and managerial R & D capacities.
2. Re-orient professional values and norms along with improved knowledge and skills.
3. Link individual with organizational capacities, for example through institutionalized mechanisms for interdisciplinary teamwork.
4. Combine human resource capacities with necessary physical, financial, and other resources.
5. Translate increased capacity into improved performance, considering relevant environmental and motivational factors.

These five premises formed the heart of the collaborative programme for PR & D capacity development. The programme was intended to be used as a platform for documenting and sharing cases of action learning through a network of projects and participants in India, Nepal, Sri Lanka, Bangladesh, and Bhutan. Moreover, the programme was envisioned as a strategic pilot test for developing regional capacity in Asia and for developing world at large.

Given the nature of PR & D and drawing on our earlier experiences, we believed that an effective capacity development initiative needs to have five key qualities. It should be:

1. *Integrated* – combining various learning methods and communication channels.
2. *Grounded* – providing hands-on experience through actual field research.
3. *Interactive* – allowing joint learning among participants and with their mentors, work supervisors, and colleagues.
4. *Continuous* – engaging in a series of cumulative, rather than one-time learning events.
5. *Reflective* – introducing self-, peer- and external-critiquing mechanisms.

With these conceptual and methodological elements in mind, the organization of the initiative is set out according to a theory of change – an envisioned pathway for capacity strengthening, outlining expected changes in PR & D capacities and performance through a deliberate strategy based on the above five elements is done. The details are given in the section entitled **How capacity development was pursued**. But before doing so, the partners and participants are introduced.

Partners and participants

At the forefront of this collaborative effort were two of South Asia's leading organizations in PR & D capacity development and its application to CBNRM: NEPAN and LI-BIRD. Meanwhile, CIP-UPWARD played a strategic role in overall programme coordination, partnership brokering, and providing PR & D expertise support (Box 5). Through a co-funding arrangement, IDRC and the International Fund for Agricultural Development (IFAD) extended key financial and technical assistance. However, it is being emphasized that the capacity development initiative was made possible through a network of over 30 organizations, both in and outside South Asia, whose staff contributed to the programme in various ways – as facilitators and resource people, mentors, advisers, and external reviewers. This turned out to be a key feature of the whole initiative and contributed to its achievements.

Box 5. Key partners in the capacity development project

UPWARD is an Asian regional network of agricultural scientists and development specialists supporting participatory approaches in root crop R & D. Since 1990, the network has engaged in collaborative field projects with over 40 institutions in China, Indonesia, Nepal, Pakistan, Sri Lanka, Philippines, and Vietnam. In seeking to develop capacity and promote the application of PR & D, UPWARD has combined field projects with training, publishing and information services, expertise linkage, and mentoring.

In this project, UPWARD capitalized on its own field experiences while forging alliances with two South Asian nongovernmental organizations (NGOs) that have been at the forefront of PR & D capacity development efforts in the region.

"As a network sponsored by the International Potato Center (CIP), UPWARD pursues research on capacity development as part of CIP's agenda on institutional learning for pro-poor impact. The PR & D South Asia Programme was envisioned to help CIP assess and document its contribution to capacity development among its national partners."

Dindo Campilan, UPWARD Coordinator

"LI-BIRD is a South Asian NGO whose overall goal is to capitalize on local initiatives in the conservation and utilization of biodiversity for sustainable development. Since its establishment in 1995, LI-BIRD has undertaken grassroots level projects relating to natural resource conservation and utilization, sustainable agriculture (crops, livestock, and agro-forestry), and community livelihood and development. Drawing on its field experiences, LI-BIRD has actively pursued training and advocacy, particularly in biodiversity conservation and crop improvement at national, regional, and international levels."

"LI-BIRD plans to design and pilot a regional course on PR & D/PAR/CBNRM by adapting the training design and learning materials produced by the programme, as well as by tapping resource persons from the informal network of PR & D practitioners formed by programme participants."

Pratap Shrestha, LI-BIRD Executive Director

"NEPAN is a national association of over 400 practitioners and organizations supporting capacity development and networking for participatory action R & D. Established in 1995, NEPAN focuses on a broad development agenda covering issues in agriculture, health, education, and gender. It regularly organizes PR & D-related training and seminars and maintains a resource centre to enhance access and availability of PR & D information in the country."

"NEPAN plans to use the programme's information outputs to feature PR & D concepts and methods in the quarterly magazine and working paper series produced by the organization, as well as to include PR & D in the portfolio of fee-based training/consultancy services that it has regularly provided to various client organizations in the country."

Raghav Raj Regmi, NEPAN Executive Committee Chair (2003–05)

At an initial meeting in June 2004, core staff from NEPAN, LI-BIRD, and UPWARD discussed the objectives, activities, and expected outcome of the envisioned collaborative process. Partners agreed on roles and task assignments and on the overall organizational arrangement. A memorandum of understanding was being signed to finalize the partnership and agreed on expected contributions and benefits. Another important feature of the efforts was the establishment of this shared operational plan.

At the core of the programme were the 16 organizations from five South Asian countries whose staff participated in the capacity development process. The organizations included six NGOs and five government development agencies, two universities, two national research institutes, and two international research organizations. Collectively, they contributed their R & D experience in a wide range of areas – crop production, biodiversity and forest conservation, health, nutrition, and community development. This richness gave the programme a unique character.

From the 28 people initially selected to represent 16 organizations, 23 eventually participated in the capacity development process. Each organization was represented by one or two participants. Two-thirds (64%) of the participants were 40 years old or younger, and 25% were women. The majority (68%) had master's degrees, one person had a Ph.D. degree, and the rest had bachelor's degrees or diploma-level education. Four out of five (78%) had an academic background in biophysical sciences, particularly agriculture and forestry. All in all, a very diverse group was formed.

How capacity development was pursued

Before starting the capacity development process, an inventory of existing capacity development initiatives that focused on rural development and relevant information resources was made. An assessment of the existing capacities in the region was also made.

Building on earlier efforts, responding to new opportunities

From the beginning, there was an awareness that several South Asian organizations were already engaged in training-based capacity development in various aspects of PR & D. Most of these organizations were NGOs, engaged in PR & D projects or activities, usually carried out in specific areas. Government organizations were also involved in capacity development, mainly through externally funded projects. With their heavy reliance on project-based funding, sustainability was a challenge in these organizations.

It was also found that a wide range of publications on PR & D already existed, including training manuals and resource books for both trainers and trainees. However, access to these materials in hard copy or electronic form was limited, particularly for smaller organizations and those located in remote areas. In addition, local organizations generally overlooked the importance of synthesizing and reflecting on their work, and lacked mechanisms for sharing and publishing their PR & D experiences.

For the lack of a forum for sharing PR & D experiences weak networking both within countries and in the region was seen. In particular, links between field-based NGOs and academic institutions were often non-existent. Thus, an opportunity to promote institutional mechanisms for regular backstopping and mentoring in-country and regional PR & D capacity efforts was seen.

In South Asia, thousands of R & D organizations are working on agriculture and natural resource management. Given the operational limitations of the PR & D South Asia programme (people, time, funds), it was important to determine which organizations could most effectively participate and benefit from the capacity development effort. Based on the overall programme design and the capacity development strategy used, it was realized that the most appropriate organizations were those who were,

1. Directly implementing research programmes or activities for sustainable agricultural livelihoods and natural resource management.
2. With an institutional mission and long-term agenda to support the integration of PR & D into their programmes and to provide PR & D capacity development support (e.g., training, publishing, networking) to other organizations nationally or regionally.
3. Operating locally, nationally, or regionally in South Asia (i.e., Bangladesh, Bhutan, India, Nepal, Pakistan, Sri Lanka).
4. Currently implementing R & D projects that could provide field research or practicum opportunities.
5. Able to provide counterpart funding of the cost of their participation (e.g., travel, staff time, supplies, fieldwork, allowances).

The selection of participants also made aware of the need to reach out to others whose home and work constraints stopped them from participating in the programme. For example, participants from

Pakistan had to drop out after encountering multiple administrative problems in traveling internationally. Two women participants were allowed to bring their young children to the training workshops.

Based on this preliminary work, a PR & D capacity development strategy was designed consisting of three main phases (Fig. 1) – introductory training, field research, and a summative workshop. Supporting phases included a needs assessment and follow up. In all, the process took two years.

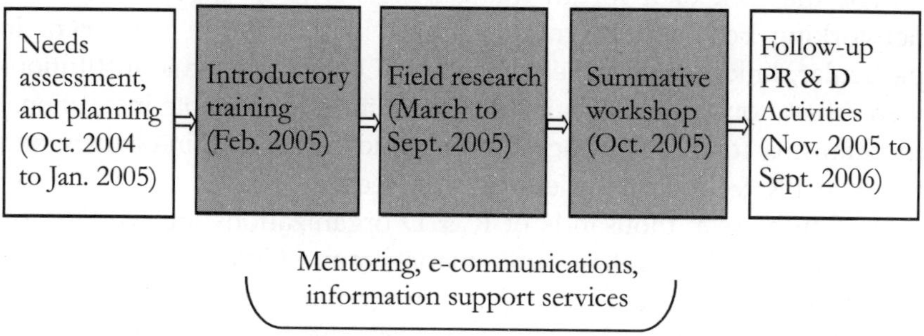

Fig. 1. Capacity development strategy

Needs assessment and planning

During the capacity needs assessment phase, expressions of interest were called for from organizations across South Asia, asking them to describe their PR & D capacity development needs and to explain how participation in the programme could help enhance their capacities. This information was used at the planning workshop to design a truly needs-based curriculum.

Among the various PR & D capacities, the most frequently cited as of interest and need to South Asian organizations were CBNRM concepts, issues and challenges in using participatory approaches, participatory technology experimentation, sharing and critiquing PR & D experiences, and monitoring and evaluation (Table 1).

Introductory training

The two-week introductory training period included classroom and field exercises based on PR & D concepts and methods.

Participants had developed draft research proposals, which they brought with them. Supervisors in the participants' own organizations provided guidance to ensure that these proposals would fit into their broader programmes. At the workshop, participants improved their

Table 1. PR & D capacity development needs of South Asian organizations.

Area of need for capacity development	Times cited (n = 28)
Understanding PR & D	
PR & D perspectives: CBNRM	20
Issues and challenges of participation in agriculture and natural resource management R & D	14
PR & D perspectives: sustainable livelihoods	12
Participation: understanding the concept	11
PR & D perspectives: user participation and building on local knowledge	11
Introduction to PR & D process and framework	10
Doing PR & D	
Case projects on PR & D: sharing, learning and critiquing PR & D experiences	14
Experimenting with technology options	14
Facilitating social/institutional/policy innovations	13
Assessment and diagnosis	12
Dissemination and scaling up	4
Enabling PR & D	
Monitoring and evaluation	14
Conceptualizing, developing and planning PR & D projects	13
Project proposal development	13
Team-building and organizational capacity development for PR & D	12
Policy development and resource mobilization	9
Networking and partnerships	7

Source: CIP-UPWARD (2006).

proposals with support from mentors and resource people or supervisors. An external panel of experts reviewed and critiqued the proposals.

For some participants, this was their first experience in proposal development. Thus, an initial challenge for the capacity development programme team was how to transform these young professionals into PR & D experts. It was decided to let mentors provide more intensive coaching by adjusting the schedule and providing more opportunities for discussion.

Field research

Participants returned to their own organizations and prepared to conduct field research based on the proposals they developed at the introductory training workshop. During this eight-month period, participants received support and guidance from their mentors through electronic communications and field visits. In addition, seminars held at their own organizations enriched the quality of their field research. Participants received constant feedback from their work supervisors and colleagues (Box 6).

Box 6. Learning in the field

A System for Rice Intensification (SRI) in Nepal

The People and Resource Dynamics Project (PARDYP) aims to generate sustainable options for natural resource management and agricultural livelihoods in five middle-mountain watersheds in the Hindu-Kush Himalayas. Implemented by the International Center for Integrated Mountain Development (ICIMOD), the project tested a system to increase rice productivity through ecologically sound management of plants, soil, water, and nutrients. Until 2004, the SRI was evaluated using on-station trials and researcher-managed on-farm trials. Participation in the PR & D programme in South Asia led PARDYP to enable farmers to test the system themselves and become agents for disseminating the innovation more widely.

In 2005–2006, participatory on-farm trials were started using the farmers' field school as the learning platform. Trials were carried out by farmer groups in 15 locations across Nepal. This was the first time PARDYP had allowed farmers to evaluate SRI directly, using their own experimental design and under local growing conditions. At each site, experimental plots were established and farmers collected weekly data on phenologic characteristics, pests and diseases, economic costs and benefits, and weather.

At the end of the 2005 season, focus group discussions and a survey were used to determine how farmers viewed the intensification system compared with traditional rice production. They found that SRI required 25% less seed and 50–60% less labour for transplanting and irrigation; it also resulted in a 40–50% increase in grain yield and a 20–25% increase in biomass production. As the researchers realized, a group-based learning approach helped farmers articulate their views and further enrich each others' knowledge gained from the experiments.

To disseminate and scale up the PR & D process, PARDYP organized sharing workshops with researchers, policymakers, and more farmers. Posters and multimedia products were developed to highlight farmers' perspectives on SRI. However, for participating farmers, there was no substitute for "seeing is believing." As they emphasized during focus group discussion and the survey, "It is easy to convince other farmers who have seen the results in the field"

M.P. Dhakal, ICIMOD, 2006.

Making Sri Lankan livelihoods less vulnerable to natural disasters

Sri Lanka was one of the countries, most affected by the 2004 Asian tsunami. Destruction, especially along the coast of the island country, included both damage to infrastructure and devastation of livelihoods. Seawater intrusion and flooding of paddy fields increased soil salinity on the limited land available to farmers in coastal communities.

Practical Action, a development NGO working in Sri Lanka since the 1980s, established a programme to apply natural resource management strategies to salvage agricultural livelihoods in the affected communities on the southern coast. The NGO saw its participation in the South Asia PR & D programme as an opportunity to conduct a participatory assessment to clarify the vulnerability situation and identify technology interventions to help local communities cope with their vulnerable condition.

The PR & D methods used included:

- Key informant interviews to assess natural resources, livelihoods, and socio-institutional set-up.
- Focus group discussions to examine types of resource use, vulnerabilities, and capacities and to validate secondary information.
- Community resource mapping to identify and characterize the natural resource base along the coastline.
- Risk mapping to identify livelihood risks and their causes.
- Field observations to monitor changes in the status of biophysical resources and management practices.
- Transect walks to establish the linkages among the activities of upstream and downstream farmers and their interrelations in terms of livelihood vulnerabilities.

The vulnerability assessment identified three major risks – flooding due to the very high flow rate in rivers after heavy rains in upstream areas, salinity in paddy fields with inadequate drainage systems, and conflicts due to changing land-use patterns, especially clearing of coastal forests and a shortened fallow cycle for paddy lands.

Assessment results served as key inputs to a series of stakeholder dialogues, which became a platform for bringing together representatives of agriculture, irrigation, and research agencies. For the local communities, the participatory vulnerability assessment empowered them for a better understanding of the problems and the options to seek external assistance.

Among the concrete actions resulting from the assessment and planning exercise were:

- 30 farmers initiated experiments to evaluate rice varieties tolerant to salinity.
- The irrigation department provided technical input in the construction of flood-control structures.
- The local government resolved to strictly reinforce policies on environmental conservation, especially those prohibiting coastal deforestation.

R.H. Weragoda and V.S.M. Hettigge, Practical Action, Sri Lanka, 2006.

During this phase, the PR & D programme's secretariat regularly provided information support to participants through a dedicated website and e-mail communication. There were many problems related to field research for the secretariat to resolve – delayed allocation of funding, transportation bottlenecks, and slow transfer of allowances. The frequent contact not only made the fieldwork more effective, it also helped strengthen ties and enhanced communications with the programme team.

For some participants who had little experience interacting with communities, the PR & D research gave them the opportunity to understand real-life issues. At the end of the research period, Bhutanese participants commented,

How farmers think and feel about their irrigation systems is now known. In the routine work, one did not get the opportunity to interact very much with farmers. Now one can be confident and happy to have the opportunity to learn more about their actual livelihood issues.

Summative workshop

Participants attended another group learning activity, this time bringing their experiences and insights from their recently completed fieldwork. As expected, the discussions were now more firmly grounded in reality. During the one-week event, mentors and the rest of the programme team recognized the need to focus learning support on data analysis and reporting.

During the week, participants presented their research findings at a seminar with a large audience of PR & D practitioners and experts. Some admitted that the PR & D South Asia programme made them "come out of the shackles" and face an audience with confidence. In addition to presenting their findings, participants prepared action plans for follow-up PR & D activities based on prior inputs from their supervisors and colleagues. At the same time, their research reports were sent for critiquing by a panel of external reviewers. Thus, all proposals were very thoroughly assessed.

Follow-up PR & D implementation

Participants knew that the summative workshop marked not the end, but the beginning of a longer-term process of continuous learning and capacity development. The action plans served as the instrument for initiating concrete PR & D activities on their return to their organizations. It was encouraging for us to receive letters and email from participants reporting on follow-up activities they had undertaken – particularly when they shared their PR & D knowledge with their colleagues, thus promoting organization-level capacity development. This is another important feature of PR & D that will be discussed in more detail in the next section.

Participants also continued to keep in touch because they felt they needed additional capacity development support. They cited the need to learn about additional concepts and methods that they realized were crucial in addressing newer problems and opportunities. Looking back, It was felt that the follow-up phase was not adequately planned by the programme team. One could not fully respond to requests for assistance, as the programme did not allocate enough resources and time for this. This shows that capacity development requires time and, is an ongoing process.

How the programme was monitored and evaluated

A monitoring and evaluation method was designed to assess each phase of the capacity development process. The programme had an in-built mechanism for feedback through mentors, reviewers, and immediate supervisors, which enabled to systematically capture learning and also document the process and outcomes.

The monitoring and evaluation system adopted a multi-event assessment approach using various tools (Table 2). A number of questionnaires were used, complemented by classroom review exercises, panel discussions, field-visit reports, progress reports, and review forms. Monitoring progress provided feedback that was used to improve implementation of subsequent phases. It also allowed one to track learning outcomes of participants and their organizations reliance on assessments conducted by mentors, using questionnaires and standardized reporting formats, as well as those from external critics and reviewers, who assessed draft proposals and reports. Toward the end of the main phases, an evaluation was conducted to examine how PR & D capacity development changed the professional perspectives of participants and to identify contributions made to the capacities of their various organizations.

These inputs together gave a benchmark for the success of the efforts in developing a cadre of PR & D practitioners in South Asia. But it did not stop there. Subsequently, the achievements of the PR & D training and capacity development process one year after the introductory training were revised. Members of the programme team were assigned to visit participating organizations and most visits were carried out. This helped understand the application of PR & D in the day-to-day work of participants and in the regular programme operations of their organizations.

Table 2. Monitoring and evaluation events and methods.

Phase	Monitoring and evaluation events	Methods
Training needs assessment, planning and design	Assessment of capacity development needs	Questionnaire
	Profiling of participating individuals and organizations	Application forms
Introductory training (training phase 1)	Assessment of training expectations	Classroom exercise
	Module and session evaluation	Questionnaire
	Final evaluation of introductory training	Questionnaire, classroom exercise
	Mentors' evaluation of participants' learning performance	Questionnaire, training team meeting

Phase	Monitoring and evaluation events	Methods
	External reviewers' critique of draft proposals	Panel discussion
Field practicum (training phase 2)	Draft proposal review and endorsement by heads of participating organizations	Endorsement letters
	Mentors' field visit	Field visit reports
	Field research implementation	Progress reports
	Monitoring of requests for information support	Communications with programme secretariat
	Participants' evaluation of field research experience	Questionnaire
	Completion of field research	Draft field research reports
Summative workshop (training phase 3)	Assessment of workshop expectations	Classroom exercise
	Module and session evaluations	Questionnaire
	Terminal evaluation of summative workshops	Questionnaire, classroom exercise
	External audience's critiquing of research seminars	Panel discussion
General	External reviewers' critiquing of draft research reports	Review forms
	Participants' evaluation of overall capacity development process and outcomes	Questionnaire
	Mentors' evaluation of participants' overall capacity development	Questionnaire
	Mentors' self-evaluation of mentoring	Questionnaire
	Participants' evaluation of mentoring	Questionnaire
Support to post-training activities	Documentation of follow-up PR & D activities	Communications with programme secretariat
	Participants' assessment of longer-term PR & D capacity development and performance	Questionnaire, key informant interviews
	Work supervisors' assessment of contributions to organizational capacity development and performance	Key informant interviews

Source: CIP-UPWARD (2006).

Part 2: Changes, insights, and challenges

Mainstreaming the human factor in conventional research

"We can speak to any official or visitor dauntlessly now, which was not the case five years ago in the small tribal hamlet of Powerguda."

Group leader, woman's self-help group, Powerguda, Andra Pradesh, India (Sreedevi 2006)

"We now understand that the cause of erosion and gully formation is a result of rotational water management practices."

Farmers of the Lhaptshakha and Gumkam irrigation scheme, Bhutan (Dhungyel and Zangmo, 2006)

"We changed from passive listeners to active participants within 10 months of participatory development capacity building."

Participants from the Renewable Natural Resources Research Center, Bhutan (Dhungyel and Zangmo, 2006)

"Farmers, who were not receptive to new technological innovations prior to participatory capacity development, appear to have changed with the introduction of PR & D capacity development."

Participants from Assam Agricultural University, India (Sharma and Pathak 2006)

These diverse statements tell a story of change from the perspective of PR & D practitioners and the agricultural communities they worked and learned with. The PR & D South Asia programme was an action learning initiative that sought to strengthen regional capacity to use participatory processes in agriculture and natural resource management. A "two-way" approach was used, where positive changes were expected from both researchers/development workers and local people, as equal partners in the action learning process.

The PR & D capacity development initiative was not expected to be a substitute for conventional research, but it was expected that the approach elaborate on the "human purpose" of R & D. Many participating organizations were mainstream research and academic institutions with established track records in conventional R & D. The programme helped them visualize and internalize the added value of users' participation in conventional R & D.

As key outputs, the PR & D South Asia programme resulted in 16 research papers published in a volume, *Learning Participation in Action: Field Research Experiences in South Asia* (Campilan et al. 2006). Half of these papers deal with participatory technology development, while the rest are about changing social and institutional structures. Notwithstanding the differences in subject matter, the authors emphasize the inclusion of "human purpose" as a key achievement for them and the programme as a whole. Through the multi-phase and multi-stakeholder capacity development process, the value of emphasizing this new dimension was discovered.

The degree of learning through participation varied depending on participants' experiences and entry-level capacities. Those who considered the learning experience of immense benefit were usually young or in the early stages of their career, unfamiliar or newly acquainted with the concepts of participation and PR & D, and having a non-social science background.

"We never believed that we could learn from farmers," said the young engineer from Bhutan. She came to the introductory training session with barely any PR & D knowledge and experience. However, by the time she presented her research paper on community-managed irrigation schemes at the summative workshop, she exuded great confidence.

These changes – among the programme partners, participants, and local communities – are the focus of the following sections.

Learning the basics of PR & D

At the end of the two-week introductory training programme, participants were expected to have acquired basic knowledge and skills in participatory approaches to R & D, recognized PR & D's added value to participants' own work and their organizations' R & D agenda, and planned a field research activity for post-training implementation.

Before the training session, participants had prepared draft concept notes for field research in consultation with their work supervisors and mentors. This preparatory work was an effective mechanism to ensure a meaningful learning experience, first, because it established a link between participants' own work and the training process and, second, requiring participants to submit concept notes confirmed their interest and commitment to the capacity development effort. During the training, they incorporated their newly acquired knowledge and skills into a concept note, then a full proposal.

During the post-training evaluation, participants rated the entire learning content as "most useful and relevant." Among the learning activities, the field visits and exercises received the highest ratings to underscore the value of learning from "live" examples of PR & D. The session on assessment and diagnosis received the lowest rating. Participants thought there was not enough time for classroom exercises in the various methods and tools.

Learning through action in the field

At the end of the field practicum period, participants prepared a draft research report, conducted a community validation workshop at the research site and an in-house research seminar for colleagues, and discussed with their supervisors a post-training action plan for the organization.

The field research period enabled participants to develop and strengthen a wider range of PR & D knowledge, attitudes, and skills. The improved capacity that was most often cited was "effectively interacting with farmers and their communities." We were somehow surprised by this result, probably because this is already a routine task in the programme team's own work. However, many participants did not have opportunities to go into the field, or lacked interest, and sometimes were prevented from doing so by their own organizations.

For participants, formal and informal discussion sessions with colleagues and financial and logistical support from their organizations were the most important aspects of the field-based learning experience. They had more diverse views on the value of electronic and on-line information support. This could be explained by their varying degrees of access to the Internet and electronic communications. This limitation was taken care of somewhat through the mentors' on-site visit to participants.

The participant–mentor relationship, which went beyond a traditional student–supervisor relationship, created a unique environment of working together. As one of the participants expressed,

"We could talk to our mentors at any time and we have no fear in talking to them. As we got to know each other, we developed a good working relationship with mentors; they are now our friends."

The added value of mentoring became more concrete when mentors were asked by participants to act as a mediator between them and their work supervisors – either when proposing new ideas or searching for resources. For participants, the concept of mentor as "coach and adviser" contrasted with the usual "boss and judge" image they saw in their work supervisors.

Participants suggested extending the field research phase, as some were unable to complete the field activities in eight months. This was especially true for those who had to fit their activities into the local cropping calendar. This point was also raised by the external reviewers of the research reports. They noted that the limited timeframe for the field research did not give participants adequate time to collect other relevant data or undertake more in-depth analysis.

From the field to the classroom

After the fieldwork phase, participants came together again for a one-week summative workshop. Participants considered this a key opportunity to review the capacity development experience and plan follow-up activities. Evaluation results indicate that the most valuable parts of this learning event were the sessions on analysis and reporting and on sharing and critiquing before an external audience. For one third of the participants, this was their first major experience of writing a research report or doing a presentation in a seminar. After the seminar, participants were proud to have successfully handled questions and criticism from the audience.

The main purpose of action planning was to identify strategies and activities for sustaining PR & D capacity development. It was the main workshop output that participants brought home, as a PR & D roadmap for themselves and their organizations (Box 7). The action plans were to include the following key features – build on earlier outcomes of the organization's participation in the PR & D South Asia programme, facilitate organizational-level capacity development for PR & D, lead to outputs/outcomes within seven months after the summative workshop, and enable the PR & D South Asia programme to support and monitor follow up activities.

The most common types of action plans developed by participants were:

1. Preparing a paper for seminar/conference presentation.
2. Preparing a paper for journal/volume publication.
3. Conducting in-house/partners' training on PR & D.
4. Conducting an in-house/partners' workshop on PR & D planning or review.
5. Developing a PR & D publication (e.g., manual, guide) for use by their organization or partners.
6. Compiling PR & D information resources (e.g., database, directory).
7. Developing a proposal for follow-up PR & D field research.

Box 7. Immediate results for participating organizations: case examples

"Sri Lanka was one of the countries most affected by the 2004 tsunami. Coupled with depletion of natural resources, the environment and landscape of coastal communities changed, making them more vulnerable to natural events. The participatory vulnerability assessment we conducted was helpful in understanding and identifying technology interventions by our NGO. It also helped bring stakeholders – government agencies, research institutes, NGOs, and community organizations – to joint agreement on the coping mechanisms. A concrete outcome was getting the irrigation department to extend technical assistance to the farming community to address the problem of salinity in their rice paddies."

R.L. Weragoda and V.S.M. Hettige, Practical Action, Sri Lanka, personal communication, *2006*

"My PR & D project illustrated the need to understand community forestry beyond single-purpose protection of forests. It made my organization recognize the need to understand community livelihoods and adopt a balanced approach in conserving biodiversity and improving livelihoods through productive forest management."

K.P. Acharya, Department of Forest Research and Survey, Nepal, personal communication, *2006*

"Farmers' participation in the early stage of evaluating sweet potato germplasm guided researchers in identifying clones to include in formal varietal development and release. Integrating farmers' selection criteria and varietal preferences helped lead the research process toward varieties with greater potential for local acceptability. Since the time this field

> research was conducted, three of these clones have been entered in the government's formal variety release scheme."
>
> *S. Attaluri and S.K. Rath, Centro Internacional de la Papa and Orissa State Government, India,* personal communication, *2006*
>
> "Our research institute had earlier proven the labour-saving potential of mechanical maize planting, but this was only on-station. We asked ourselves, 'How will this technology fare in farmers' fields, with farmers using it, and what do they have to say about this technology?' Thus my field research focused on the participatory evaluation of mechanical planting. The Department of Agriculture realized how this was helpful in understanding farmers' adoption or rejection of technologies. My department decided to learn more about how to do PR & D by doing more of it! Our next activity is to apply participatory technology evaluation for tomato varieties."
>
> *M.A.R. Bhuiyan, Department of Agricultural Extension, Bangladesh,* personal communication, *2006*

Beyond capacity development: what happened next?

For 12 months after the summative workshop, the programme secretariat continued to monitor participants' implementation of follow-up PR & D activities. The programme also provided support activities to participating organizations – consultation by electronic communication, distribution of information, and technical and funding assistance to scale up and institutionalize capacity development. Toward the end of this period, a questionnaire was sent to participants to solicit information on their experience in implementing PR & D action plans. This was supplemented by another round of field visits by selected members of the programme team.

All the participating organizations reported that they had undertaken activities that built on their learning experience in the PR & D South Asia programme. Most (83%) were next-season or cycle experiments and field assessments to follow-up on the research they carried out during the main programme phase. For example:

1. The Ministry of Agriculture in Bhutan conducted a participatory market chain assessment to complement the seed systems study it had done earlier. This enabled farmers to identify and refine on-farm innovations based on market requirements for product quantity and quality.

2. India's International Crops Research Institute for the Semi-Arid Tropics replicated its original *Pongamia* experiment in two additional villages, where a community-based water energy project was initiated. The community-based approach piloted during the PR & D South Asia programme was also used to initiate a partnership with the National Oil Seeds and Vegetable Oils Development Board in a project to recover "wastelands" by planting *Jatropha* and *Pongamia* trees.
3. The Horticulture Research and Development Institute in Sri Lanka conducted a second round of participatory on-farm trials to validate the results of the previous season's experiments. Subsequently, this participatory approach was adopted by the institute to replace the long-established system of variety adaptation trials.
4. The Nepali NGO, Forest Action, together with an international partner organization, organized an international course on community forestry, which included findings from its earlier documentation study.

Three-quarters of participating organizations also prepared project proposals and programme plans to mobilize resources for PR & D, and 25% obtained grants within one year. The CIP team in India, developed and submitted two research proposals on participatory evaluation and promotion of high-vitamin A sweet potato varieties. The participant from the Green Foundation in India led the development and establishment of a new local NGO, with a focus on sustainable and organic farming.

For participants from Bangladesh, more significant fact was that the capacity development efforts sensitized them and their organizations to the value of users' participation:

> "Although research findings did not significantly contribute to new technical knowledge on seedling/sapling production, poor women and other institutional stakeholders were exposed to the PR & D approach. This experience made us recognize that we are equal partners in assessing strengths and weaknesses of two methods of nursery development. Through the PR & D experience, participating organizations learned to accept a different view of conventional research."
>
> *M.A. Motalib, Department of Agricultural Extension, Bangladesh,* personal communication, *2006.*

> "The technology evaluation was still mainly a researcher-designed and managed experiment. It could have been a more effective platform for joint learning if farmers' cross-visits and an end-of-season evaluation were conducted. But all is not lost; it is only the first step. The important thing is that the crucial first step has been taken and another step will soon be taken – with lessons learned from the first step guiding the way."
>
> *M.A.R. Bhuiyan, Department of Agricultural Extension, Bangladesh,* personal communication, *2006.*

Evidence of these PR & D initiatives can be found in the various reports, papers, and publications produced by participating individuals and their colleagues. Among these were papers presented at international conferences by the Department of Forestry Research and Survey in Nepal and articles published by Practical Action in Sri Lanka and the State Government of Orissa in India.

Responses to the questionnaire revealed various outcomes not only for individuals, but also for their organizations. Participants reported increased use of PR & D by their organizations and an enhanced PR & D capacity among their colleagues and partners (Table 3).

Table 3. Organizational outcomes of participation in the PR & D South Asia programme.

Outcome	No. of organizations ($n = 16$)
Increased PR & D capacity of colleagues	11
Increased use of PR & D in activities of the organization	11
Increased PR & D capacity of partners	10
Greater support for PR & D from supervisors/managers	7
Better evidence of the organization's impact on local communities	7
Increased allocation of the organization's financial/human/other resources for PR & D	6
Improved linkages with other individuals/organizations with PR & D expertise	6
Enhanced achievement of goals/objectives/targets	5
Increased recognition/awards received	3
Increased availability of external resources/support for PR & D	1

Source: CIP-UPWARD (2006).

Despite the progress, various constraints were encountered by participating organizations in improving their PR & D capacity and performance. Going by the list (Table 4) there was the need to build a critical mass of staff members with PR & D capacities; one or two people participating in the programme proved to be inadequate to influence the organization's overall PR & D capacity development. Another frequently cited constraint was an organization's inability to secure additional funding to support subsequent PR & D activities.

Table 4. Constraints to improving organizations' PR & D capacity and performance.

Constraint	% of organizations ($n = 16$)
Need to build a critical mass of staff members with PR & D capacity	50
PR & D project terminated and no new funding available	42
Current project does not have flexibility to channel funds for PR & D	33
Current project was originally planned without PR & D component and it is not flexible enough to integrate PR & D mid-way in the implementation	33
Limited opportunities for communicating and linking with other organizations	33
Difficult to travel to PR & D field sites in remote locations	33
Conflicts among project partners	17
Limited awareness on PR & D by heads of organizations	17
Frequent staff turnover	17
Heavy staff workloads resulting in R & D activities being deprioritized	8
Participating farmers are extremely poor, with very little time and other resources to participate in PR & D	8
Limited availability of PR & D reading and promotional materials	8

Source: CIP-UPWARD (2006).

Seven heads of organizations were also interviewed to assess improvements in the PR & D performance of their staff members who participated in the programme and to find out how these staff members contributed to strengthening organizational-level PR & D capacity. Staff members were observed to have performed better in terms of critical thinking, self-confidence, and teamwork. They were also credited for using their individual capacities to improve organizational capacities in PR & D, mainly by sharing what they learned with colleagues and partners and by reinforcing and highlighting existing organizational PR & D practices (Table 5).

Table 5. Improvement in participants' PR & D performance and their contribution to organizational PR & D capacity as assessed by their work superiors.

Categories	No. of organizations ($n = 7$)
Participants' improved PR & D performance	
Demonstrate critical thinking	4
Greater self-confidence to accomplish assigned PR & D tasks	2
More effective team worker/builder	2
Participants' contribution to organizational capacity in P&D Share with colleagues what they learned from the project	4
Reinforce existing organizational practices in PR & D	3
Share with partners what they learned from the project	3
Increase the organization's interest to learn from others' experiences	2
Help promote shared understanding of PR & D by all members of the organization	2
Help organization to develop technical and other outputs more relevant to end-users	2
None	1

Source: CIP-UPWARD (2006).

Dr. Mangalika Nugewella, supervisor of the participants from the Horticultural Research and Development Institute (HORDI) in Sri Lanka had this to say:

"A significant achievement by HORDI staff participating in the PR & D programme was upscaling potato seed production to nearly 300 farmers. PR & D also demonstrated that participatory group learning is more effective than the variety adoptive trial (VAT) conventionally used by our institute. In the latter case, we provided farmers with a package of technologies and expected them to follow instructions. However in PR & D, researchers involve farmers from the beginning to end of the trials, as equal partners in the learning process. It has brought farmers and researchers together more closely, which was not the practice under the VAT system.

However, I believe that the success of PR & D depends on changing the mindset of some senior officials in the Department of Agriculture, which the participants are unable to do alone. To achieve this, we need to organize a sharing workshop with senior researchers and bureaucrats to secure their support for PR & D. But a workshop would not be enough. It needs to be followed up by field projects that would aim to demonstrate how PR & D can enhance the effectiveness of our agricultural research programmes."

When the heads of organizations were asked about constraints to further scale up and the institutionalization of PR & D (Table 6), they pointed out that they tend to lose staff with strong PR & D capacities, because they are often temporary employees (i.e., project based or contractual workers). This was the case, for example, with two young participants from the Forum for Rural Welfare and Agricultural Reform for Development and the International Center for Integrated Mountain Development, both in Nepal. Their project-based employment contracts expired soon after they participated in the PR & D South Asia programme.

Table 6. Key constraints to and opportunities for further strengthening organization-level PR & D capacity, as viewed by heads of organizations.

Categories	No. of organizations (n = 7)
Key constraints in strengthening organizational capacity	
Staff with strong PR & D capacities have project-based/contractual employment status	4
It takes longer to generate tangible outcomes from PR & D	3
Limited resources to support efforts to develop PR & D capacities of more staff	3
Key opportunities in strengthening organizational capacity	
Plan and adopt a more formal strategy for organizational capacity development	4
Introduce mechanisms for internal mentoring	4
Consciously seek to translate individual into organizational level capacities	3
Allocate more resources for field projects that serve as vehicles for PR & D	3
Identify younger staff with potential to lead PR & D capacity development	2

Source: CIP-UPWARD (2006).

Partners in the PR & D South Asia programme also undertook follow-up activities during the twelve-month period after the summative workshop. Among the significant accomplishments were:

1. *LI-BIRD* – Prepared a concept note, with UPWARD, for a follow-up initiative to conduct a scoping study on PR & D capacity development efforts in South Asia. This is intended as an intermediate step in further scaling-up and institutionalization efforts. Together with UPWARD, LI-BIRD also developed a PR & D project proposal to promote sweet potatoes for nutrition and livelihood improvement in South Asia; it was submitted to the Gates Foundation.
2. *NEPAN* – Negotiated with Norwegian partners to conduct customized PR & D training for the staff of a forestry college in Nepal. NEPAN also facilitated a series of learning workshop on curriculum development to support follow-up training by Nepalese organizations participating in the programme.
3. *UPWARD* – Adapted the programme's curriculum for an international training course on participatory research and extension, organized annually since 2005 by the International Rice Research Institute. UPWARD also adapted the capacity development strategy in a new IDRC project for organizations engaged in research on urban poverty and environment.
4. *IDRC* – Programme experience informed the design and implementation of two new regional capacity development initiatives in Southeast Asia: adaptive learning for CBNRM (*see* chapter 3) and learning to use evaluation in CBNRM capacity development (mentioned in chapter 1).
5. *IFAD* – Programme experience guided similar PR & D capacity development efforts for IFAD investment programmes in China, Lao PDR, and Vietnam under the "Participatory Research for Development in the Uplands" project implemented by CIP-UPWARD and the International Center for Tropical Agriculture. The programme has also helped IFAD find South Asian resource people and mentors for the soon-to-be launched National Agricultural Technology Project in Bangladesh.

Improving the way capacity development is done: insights and challenges

Result-oriented capacity development

The programme successfully field-tested the effectiveness of a PR & D capacity development strategy, designed and implemented through multistakeholder participation and a needs-driven learning agenda.

Compared with previous efforts by other organizations, the programme's capacity-development strategy can be distinguished by its use of a sustained learning process rather than a one-time event; direct links between classroom learning and field immersion; customized support through flexible group learning, individual mentoring, and access to information resources; and joint contribution and benefits for stakeholders, rather than a one-way, dole-out type investment.

Monitoring and evaluation of the programme revealed that it strengthened capacities to understand, work, and enable PR & D – although there was much less evidence of the latter. Participants also developed generic PR & D capacities, such as greater self-confidence and skill in undertaking fieldwork and making public presentations. However, as participants suggested, there is a need to address continuing capacity gaps and weaknesses particularly in data analysis and reporting.

Some key components of the capacity development strategy need further review and refinement. Although mentoring is one of its most innovative features, the pool of field-tested concepts and methods needed to equip mentors to perform their role effectively is still limited. The limited contribution of advanced electronic communications – particularly through web-based tools – to participants' learning outcomes suggests that future investments in these newer media should be carefully assessed.

Institutionalization and scaling up

Follow-up showed that the process of PR & D learning and application extended beyond the summative workshop. In the succeeding twelve months, participating organizations independently launched their own efforts to sustain and expand PR & D capacity development and practice. More could probably have been achieved if the programme had also maintained its level of capacity development support; however, inability to cope with the additional resource requirements became a limiting factor. The time horizon was clearly underestimated.

Both participants and their work superiors reported that a process of transforming individual into organizational capacity had emerged. However, this did not occur uniformly across all organizations. A longer timeframe is needed to strengthen organizational capacity, a critical mass of PR & D supporters and advocates (beyond the one or two people who had participated in the programme) must be created, and interventions specifically aimed at heads of organizations, who play a strategic role in organizational capacity development, may be required.

Nonetheless, the programme's contribution to PR & D institutionalization and scaling up remains noteworthy. This is a result of a number of factors. First, the process of planning and implementing PR & D capacity development started and ended with organizations, i.e., organizations served as the primary unit for selecting programme participants, and follow-up action plans focused on activities to be undertaken by organizations. Second, we made a proactive effort to seek co-investment from participating organizations, through matching cash and in-kind contributions. Third, we designed the learning activities to involve and require input from work superiors and colleagues of the participating individuals.

There was significant diversity among participants, who represented a cross-section of South Asian organizations engaged in PR & D. However, in further promoting institutionalization and scaling up, a more comprehensive scoping study would be useful to identify and engage with strategic partners in the region.

Tracking the outcomes of capacity development

The programme benefited from a deliberately planned and pro-actively implemented monitoring and evaluation scheme as evidenced by the amount and relevance of information available on the process, outputs, and outcomes of capacity development. The validity and reliability of our monitoring and evaluation was increased by gathering data from various sources and perspectives (e.g., participants, work superiors, mentors, and external reviewers).

To further enhance the role of monitoring and evaluation of learning for effective capacity development, the following improvements are suggested – carry out more in-depth documentation of improvements in capacity and performance over a longer-time frame; employ a richer mix of methods to capture more qualitative dimensions, emerging relationships, and contributions of factors and actors; address the cost-effectiveness of the resource-intensive nature of the programme's PR & D capacity development strategy.

Finally, although monitoring and evaluation helped establish a rich pool of information on the experience, adequate time and resources was not allocated for more meaningful knowledge synthesis, distillation, and dissemination. Information on our key outputs and outcomes is potentially of wider usefulness, especially to those engaged in similar capacity development initiatives. Thus, a key challenge remains to continue learning from the experience and explore opportunities to share it within a broader community of PR & D practice.

Conclusions

It was hypothesized that PR & D capacity development must have five key qualities for it to be effective; it must be integrated, grounded, interactive, continuous, and reflective. The synergic effects of these five qualities were empirically demonstrated during the programme.

The programme experience underscored two additional qualities that are also increasingly highlighted in recent literature on capacity development. First is the overarching learning mode that drives and frames the capacity development process. Joint adaptive learning is the essence of capacity development, especially in the context of PR & D. Blueprint-style planning, applied rigidly and in every detail, works less effectively. This explained the disappointing results of capacity development programmes in developing countries in a review of 20 cases by the European Centre for Development Policy and Management (Watson 2006).

Second is the systemic nature of capacity and capacity development. While specific competencies or types of capabilities are after spoken about, capacity development is the overall ability of a system to create value (Morgan 2006). PR & D cannot succeed through the effort of a single individual or of several individuals acting independently. In the same way, developing PR & D capacity involves acquiring and mobilizing different attributes of a system – whether a project team, a large organization, or a network of partners.

In summing up the PR & D programme experience, the reflections of Gelia Castillo, one of the mentors and senior programme advisers (Castillo and Campilan 1999) are cited:

"Consistent with the view that PR & D is not a substitute, but a socially significant value-added to conventional research, all the case projects in the PR & D South Asia Programme indicate that good technical (biophysical) research is almost always necessary. The technical components are essential to the rigor, relevance, and empirical evidence required for PR & D to be both technically sound and participatory. PR & D should not mean "lacking in rigor".

In every case, participation played its role in the elaboration of the human dimensions of the research, whether the project was about mung bean or social exclusion. In other words, the papers validate the concept that agriculture and natural resource management research is ultimately about people, about human development and the choices which they should be able to make.

There is also no question about the value of PR & D capacity development, which is anchored in actual projects carried out in a learning-by-doing mode, encouraged by a mentor. But because PR & D is still very much in progress, every opportunity must be used to learn from the concepts, the practices, and the processes in order to contribute to the robustness of the approach. What happens to PR & D when it is translated from rhetoric and ideology to practice [Box 8]?

Box 8. What next for PR & D? The case of traditional knowledge on seed storage in India

"Effective seed management practices play an important role in safeguarding food security and achieving self-sufficiency in good-quality seeds for small and marginal farming communities. In India, pulses constitute a major nutritional value in the dietary system of resource-poor farmers. However, pulses attract pests during storage because the protein content is high.

Realizing this growing problem, the GREEN Foundation conducted participatory seed storage research with women farmers. As a result, traditional seed storage practices have been standardized and replicated across Karnataka State. The PR & D experience validated the valuable knowledge possessed by farmers and its potential for addressing seed storage constraints faced by wider farming communities.

We at GREEN Foundation believe that traditional knowledge should be put in the public domain. However this could also raise issues about legal protection given to local knowledge; and biopiracy of knowledge without benefits accruing to the local community.

While espousing PR & D, the GREEN Foundation is deeply concerned about the implications of opening up the repository of traditional knowledge for commercial exploitation. How can the interest of vulnerable farming communities be protected, in the context of growing globalization of knowledge sharing? This unanswered question haunts us."

— *G. Krishna Prasad and Dr. Vanaja Ramprasad*
GREEN Foundation, personal communication, *2006*

What are the yields from the application of participatory tools? Do they really make a difference? If they do, what difference do they make? What value-added do they account for? What tools are particularly suited for which types of information needed in the project?

In seeking to strengthen and expand a regional community of PR & D practitioners in South Asia, the following insights are worth keeping in mind:

PR & D promises at least five attributes – participation, research, development, focus on less favorable areas, and for the benefit of those who have less in life. Because these requirements are quite onerous, not everyone will be attracted to this type of professional undertaking. A higher level of commitment will be required. How many of the participating researchers will want to pursue PR & D as a preferred research approach?

On the other hand, farmers in all of the research sites are not tradition-bound, even in experimenting with traditional methods. Some experimented with innovations; others were not as enthused. Follow-up studies are much needed to see whether any of the introduced technologies or institutional arrangements have taken root and what adaptations were made to improve goodness of fit between new technologies both biophysical and socio-economic and the existing circumstances.

PR & D by its very nature is not for every researcher and for every research project. PR & D is demanding and is intensive in terms of time, human relations, facilitation skills, creativity under unpredictable circumstances, social sensitivity, hands-on engagement in addition to research competence. PR & D is research and therefore research competence is the core competence required. But most of all, PR & D "promises" much more than the conventional research project, whether in the biophysical or social sciences.

PR & D is not for the faint-hearted, but the rewards for the researcher are immense in terms of beyond-science insights; deeper elucidation of the human dimension; a sense of humility because real life is more complex even if more fascinating than the research proposal one has written. The greatest challenge lies in the improved prospect for achieving difficult objectives. This remains to be demonstrated in larger measure. Simply put, PR & D must deliver on its promises."

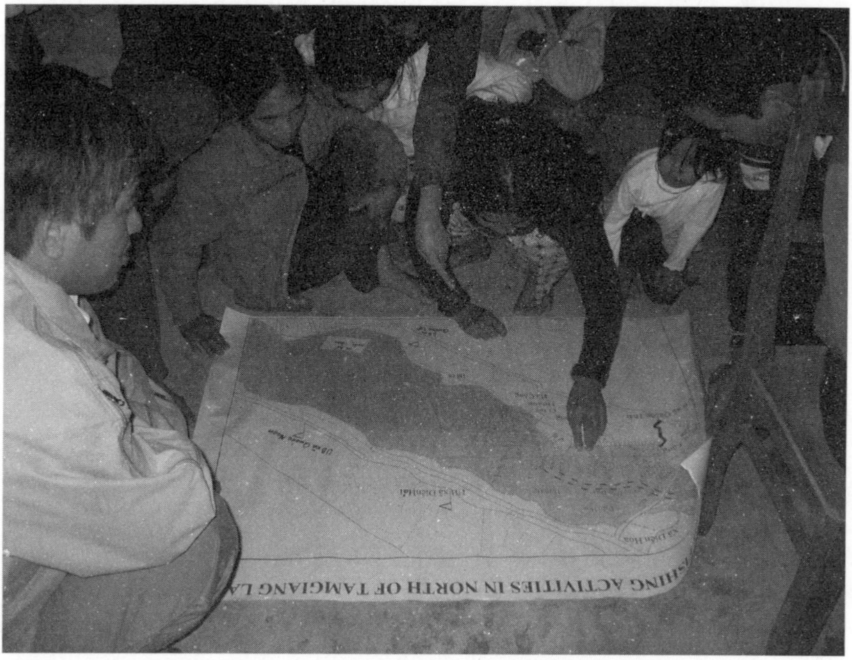

Women villagers discuss the lagoon zoning plan.
Photo: AllinCBNRM archive.

3

Adaptive Learning: From Isang Bagsak to the ALL in CBNRM Programme

Maria Celeste H. Cadiz and Winifredo B. Dagli

Part 1: About the case study

Rural communities and field researchers aiming to achieve sustainable management of the environment need to adapt to rapidly changing contexts of rural poverty and resource degradation. This capacity is called adaptive learning or, adaptive management. Adaptive learning is based on the premise that *learning* from their experiences empowers participants to respond more effectively to new uncertainties, enabling them to change old ways of doing things and allowing them to make better decisions in managing the natural resource base.

Thus learning is a knowledge enterprise where new knowledge is generated from experiences, shared through formal and non-formal channels of communication, stored, and relearned in a creative fashion. However, this is easier said than done. How this cyclical process takes place in the context of Community-Based Natural Resource Management (CBNRM), which is a social process by nature, is something that research and development agencies, academic institutions, and learning centres should explore more deeply and document it. This will allow one to understand whether contextual factors make learning possible or not.

The Adaptive Learning and Linkages in Community-Based Natural Resource Management programme (ALL in CBNRM) and its earlier phases, the Isang Bagsak programme, have tried to provide answers to this question by facilitating a regional programme in adaptive learning for CBNRM researchers and practitioners in Southeast Asia.

Isang Bagsak and ALL in CBNRM apply an innovative learning model that allows learners to consolidate and synthesize their collective knowledge and experiences in participatory research and development (PR & D), to derive pragmatic CBNRM principles that can be applied to changing situations and to improve past actions.

The cry "isang bagsak!" or literally, "one bang!", followed by a single resounding, united clap of hands or slap on the table by participants in a meeting was a common occurrence in learning workshops of this capacity building and networking programme of the same name. This practice, which had become commonplace in participatory meetings popularized by nongovernmental organizations (NGOs) in the Philippines, indicates agreement on collective decisions made through dialogue. It is also used as confirmation of the actions undertaken or envisioned by a group or subgroup. The cry "isang bagsak!" was thus adopted as an appropriate name for a programme focusing on participatory development communication (PDC) in natural resource management (NRM).

This programme has evolved constantly. True to the philosophy of PDC as a collective process of learning and communication, it continues to do so and add value to community-based practices and programmes in NRM in the region. NRM refers to a wide variety of livelihood activities of people who rely primarily on nature, mainly agriculture, but also aquaculture and fisheries, forestry and agroforestry, and use of marine and coastal resources.

Since its inception as a pilot initiative in 2001, involving three learning groups representing field-based projects in Cambodia, Uganda, and Vietnam, the programme has advocated a communication approach to enhance the work and impact of NRM field researchers and practitioners. It has walked its learning participants (teams of researchers and practitioners) through a cycle of 10 steps in PDC. PDC is centred on the assumptions that the involvement of the NRM community in research and development will increase its impact and that this is, in essence, a communication process. PDC should, therefore, inform the practices of NRM researchers and practitioners as they work with farmers, fishers, and other members of the community toward better livelihoods and care of the natural environment.

In its most recent period under the new name ALL in CBNRM, the assumption of the centrality of communication in research and development remains. However, the programme has expanded to embrace additional perspectives and methods of PR & D, including social and gender analysis, adaptive and social learning, participatory rural appraisal, participatory action research, and participatory monitoring and evaluation. The capacity-building programme is now run by five partner organizations and coordinated by the University of the Philippines Los Baños, College of Development Communication (UPLB CDC). The other four partner organizations are the Community-Based Natural Resource Management Learning Center (CBNRM LC), the Centro Internacional de la Papa's Users' Perspectives With Agricultural Research and Development (CIP-UPWARD) Asian network, the International Institute of Rural Reconstruction (IIRR), and the Regional Community Forestry Training Center for Asia and the Pacific (RECOFTC).

What and how are changes taking place

Charting the changes that the Isang Bagsak – ALL in CBNRM programme has achieved is not an easy task because of its multiple dimensions. Tracking these changes is also a challenge, given that capacity development is seldom a linear process.

Briefly, the multiple dimensions of change cover three broad fields of action and interaction. The first concerns the individual learning processes of those directly involved in the programme. The second concerns the gains made by the project teams and their organizations as a result of participating. Last, but not least, are the adaptations of the communities with whom the CBNRM researchers and practitioners are working. It is assumed that improved communication contributes to local people's capacities to cope with challenges in their livelihoods, natural resources, and communities. This human and social dimension of people's capacities is often overlooked in development work that emphasizes economic indicators and science-based NRM practices.

Evidence of change is gathered and analysed. For this chapter, a thematic analysis and review of both basic and processed research outputs (key texts) has been undertaken generated by the current programme so far. Data from Isang Bagsak Southeast Asia reports and an unpublished proposal (*Evaluating Capacity Development in ALL in CBNRM Study* by Tirol et al. 2007) were reviewed and analysed. These were collected through surveys, fieldwork, and regional mid-term and final evaluation workshops held in the Philippines and Thailand.

The programme has touched and effected change among 33 learning groups including project teams, organizations, and networks – 19 in Southeast Asia, 9 in eastern and southern Africa, and 5 in western Africa – directly involving close to 300 people. These learning groups work in and with hundreds of communities. The changes observed so far vary considerably – from an appreciation of the role of communication in field-based NRM research and development to more systematic communication initiatives in projects and an integration of the PDC process in the research and development cycle of NRM field projects. Here, the attempt is to offer a preliminary analysis of the factors that have contributed to change. Using Paulo Freire's (1970) key concept of praxis, identification of the types of learning groups best at transforming and adopting PDC is tried.

Changes in programme organization

The Isang Bagsak programme was initially an IDRC pilot initiative (2001–2003). It involved two experts in PDC as facilitator and resource person and one learning group each in Cambodia, Uganda, and Vietnam. A second phase (2003–2005) was developed and implemented in Southeast Asia and coordinated by the UPLB CDC. In parallel, the pilot stage expanded from Uganda to other parts of eastern and southern Africa and a site in West Africa. The current ALL in CBNRM programme in Southeast Asia (2006–2008) has evolved into a partnership of five organizations aiming to develop a centre of excellence in CBNRM. This expansion from a small pilot project to a multi-organizational community of practice in six years represents a remarkable evolution.

In the broader context of CBNRM practice in Southeast Asia, ALL in CBNRM now includes various institutions that have developed regional capacities in CBNRM research and capacity building, from both sectoral and intersectoral perspectives. Some of these institutions have developed training programmes and materials relevant to one or more methodological approaches, e.g., PR & D, participatory monitoring and evaluation, PDC, social and gender analysis. Sometimes, duplication has occurred. The current collaboration between regional institutions in the design and delivery of ALL in CBNRM allows for integration of these approaches, enables the pooling of resources and materials, and facilitates the development of synergies.

The process of bringing five organizations together to collaborate in offering the ALL in CBNRM programme is no mean task. Although these organization share complementary if not similar approaches to rural development through CBNRM, they are all fully engaged in countless other activities within their mandates. Besides offering non-formal learning programmes, they also offer formal academic degree programmes or courses or engage in field-based research, sometimes both. Transcending distance through electronic communication, their periodic and somewhat rare opportunities for face-to-face meetings have been valuable, fruitful occasions for synergy and ongoing programme innovation.

Box 9. Reflections of the implementing partners on their experience in the ALL in CBNRM programme

"We are happy to be part of the programme and contribute our small bit to running it. Here, we are able to learn and share our experiences in knowledge management, and further enhance what we've been doing in the past … . There remains much to do in the area of natural resource management … . The issue is not just a matter of management, but the urgency of preserving life, in the contemporary challenge of a changing climate." – *Elmer Ferrer, CBNRM LC*

"RECOFTC has been working in CBNRM for a long time and has its own network of CBNRM practitioners in the region. Our joining the programme is a way for us to get innovative ideas for people to learn about CBNRM, particularly on e-learning as an option. We found the invitation from UPLB CDC to join the programme as a good opportunity to learn how to run the e-learning component of the programme."

"In terms of working with CBNRM, e-learning is a challenge. We need to reconsider the context that we would like to focus on. Different countries have different settings, and the approach should take into consideration how e-learners can elaborate on their respective contexts. The challenge is facilitating an exchange between e-learners from different cultures sharing different experiences and lessons learned. In this process, they are able to form a regional network as well as local networks." – *Ronnakorn Triraganon, RECOFTC*

"IIRR was very excited when it joined the initiative. It has been a good opportunity to enhance our own CBNRM initiatives. Our interest is in enhancing partnerships involving learning, sharing and working together in CBNRM." – *Emily Monville Oro, IIRR*

"What is unique in ALL in CBNRM is that each partner brings its own sectoral interests into the partnership – such as forestry, coastal resources, and agriculture – yet the learning process has encouraged us to recognize cross-country challenges in CBNRM, both conceptual and operational. Overall, this is a learning process that adds further value to what we could learn individually." – *Dindo Campilan, CIP-UPWARD*

Source: Video footages of interviews with partners during ALL in CBNRM Review, Planning and Capacity Development Workshop, 21–25 May, 2007.

The need to continuously refine and define the collaboration process is key to nurturing the partnership and achieving the CBNRM goals. Tasks and responsibilities, as well as issues and concerns that require decisions by the various institutions have to be defined and clarified. Though some challenges remain, the effectiveness in doing this is achieved.

As the programme holder, UPLB CDC has initiated the organization of all programme activities, drafted concept notes, and convened meetings among the implementing partners. The partners have acted as a "board of directors" for ALL in CBNRM, where decisions are made through a collective process.

Reflecting on their experience in ALL in CBNRM, the implementing partners are recasting their working relations beyond policymaking and have committed to moving toward more substantive sharing of responsibilities in areas relevant to ALL in CBNRM and their various organizations. For example, CIP-UPWARD has volunteered to lead in improving the research grants programme, drawing from its greater experience in this area relative to other implementing partners. Similarly, CBNRM LC, IIRR, and RECOFTC will work further on the curriculum, while UPLB CDC will continue with its interest in programme evaluation following UPWARD's lead and in improving learning modalities and knowledge management, fields in which it has treaded a bit farther than the partners.

The partners' coming together as organizations lends stability to the programme, although individual personalities come and go. At the same time, the personal relationships and trust that have been built up among its managers, mentors, facilitators, and learning group representatives act as a strong binding force for continued commitment and collective creativity.

Changes in programme content

The main aim of the programme is the adoption of a systematic, logical framework for the effective integration of participatory approaches into the research and development cycle of NRM projects. Bessette (2003, 2004) charted such a framework as a 10-step PDC process (Fig. 2).

Based on this model, the adaptive learning methods and practice of the ALL in CBNRM programme were expanded from the primary focus on PDC to 10 themes covering the main domains of PR & D in CBNRM. However, on reflection, the implementing partners noted that, in practice, they were often addressing several themes simultaneously. Bessette's linear structure was too limiting and was, thus, expanded to 13 CBNRM steps, organized into four clusters as outlined below.

Cluster 1: Establishing relationships

1. Establishing a relationship with a local community and understanding the local setting
2. Involving the community in the identification of a problem, its potential solutions, and the decision to carry out a concrete initiative
3. Identifying the various community groups and other stakeholders concerned with the identified problem (or goal) and initiative

Cluster 2: Gaining understanding

4. Understanding the roles and concepts in CBNRM.
5. Arriving at a collective understanding of the local community and the CBNRM context.
6. Enhancing the community's capacity for identifying problems and setting goals.

Cluster 3: Facilitating flow/movement

7. Understanding stakeholder relationships in a CBNRM setting.
8. Developing and implementing a participatory communication plan.
9. Enhancing processes for collective action.
10. Developing partnerships.

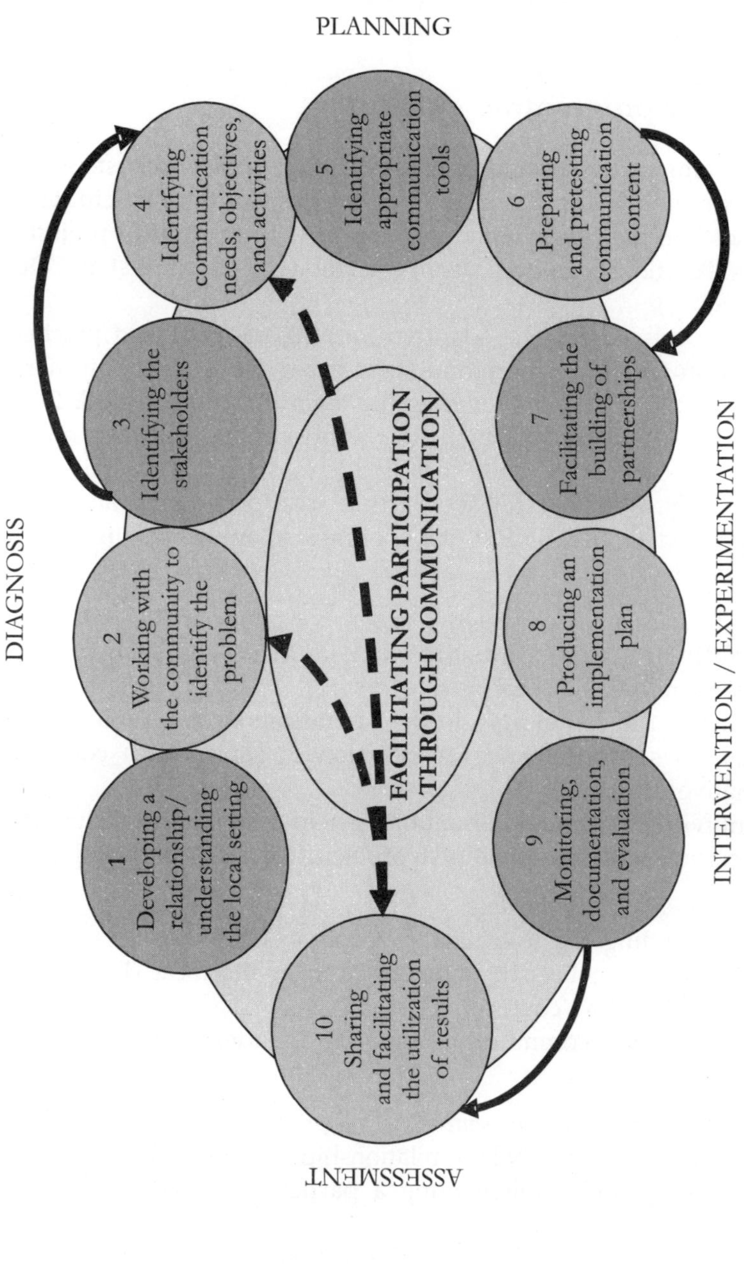

Fig. 2. The PDC process superimposed against four stages in the research and development cycle (Bessette 2003, 2004).

Cluster 4: Grounding and supporting implementation and facilitation

11. Monitoring, evaluating, and documenting CBNRM experiences.
12. Encouraging CBNRM adaptation and innovation (e.g., addressing livelihoods, vulnerabilities, climate change).
13. Participatory processes for policy change.

Changes in programme modalities

As open-learning innovations, both the Isang Bagsak and ALL in CBNRM pilot initiatives were works in progress in which ongoing improvements made the programme an adaptive learning process itself for its implementers. The programme continues to evolve, trying to improve how it serves its learning groups and, consequently, the Southeast Asian communities they work with.

In terms of methods, the Isang Bagsak project used a combination of the following approaches:

1. An introductory workshop for the in-house team.
2. Team discussion meetings.
3. Direct field application of new principles and practices learned.
4. A regional electronic forum where team discussion highlights for each PDC step or theme were posted in separate folders to exchange with other teams in the region.
5. A regional mid-term training workshop.
6. A final regional evaluation and planning workshop.

To this cycle of learning and sharing, programme facilitators added monitoring and evaluation activities as well as a component to cap the learning process by documenting the participating teams' insights and experiences and sharing them with others. This is done through a "writeshop" to develop a monograph, somewhat similar to the thesis or special problem paper required in academic degree programmes.

The Southeast Asian network facilitators also felt that more support for learning teams in the field was needed (backstopping); and this led to another adjustment in strategies for the next phase. Thus, the ALL in CBNRM programme adopted the learning gained in the Isang Bagsak programme as well as the knowledge of the new implementing partners in terms of their various capacity building and field-based programmes. This has produced synergy, which brought about additional improvements in the current programme. Three more components were added (Fig. 3):

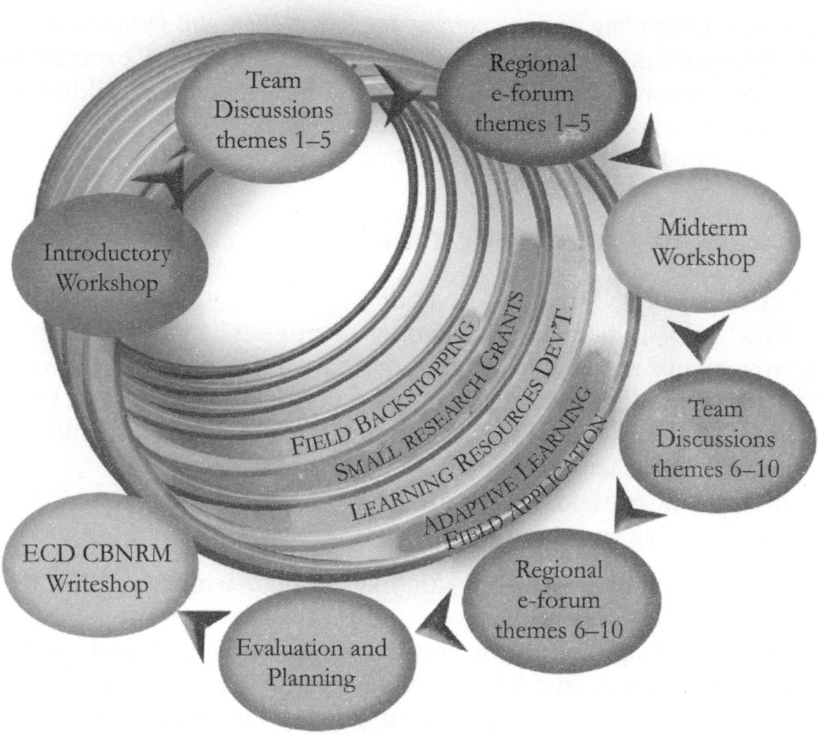

Fig. 3. The ALL in CBNRM learning modalities, with the addition of field backstopping, small research grants, and learning resources development, and adaptive learning in the field application (grafted onto the original Isang Bagsak programme design).

Small research grants

These encourage and support learning groups to test newer approaches that complement their action research. The purpose of this small grants scheme was to enable learning groups to deepen their understanding of participatory CBNRM and exercise their creativity and innovation by practicing its principles.

Knowledge banking

Mechanisms used to capture and share the new knowledge gained by ALL in CBNRM participants included distance learning, an online resource centre, face-to-face workshops, and field backstopping. Success stories, insights, lived experiences, and lessons were also captured in documents. However, few participants had time to search diligently through voluminous e-forum archives, workshop proceedings, and reference materials.

This led to the development of a more effective knowledge management strategy (Dagli 2006). The ALL in CBNRM Knowledge Bank is a repository for all content and processes generated by the programme. The system is meant to trigger innovation and meaningful knowledge sharing between and among learners in the programme. It includes a system for analyzing knowledge to reveal trends, gaps, and relationships that cut across the lived experiences of the participating groups as shared in online discussions. This process may also facilitate "double loop learning" that would increase learners' capacity to think creatively and act innovatively. More importantly, it can be a tool for theory building and mapping new research agendas.

The goal is a simple and friendly system and users can work with it whatever way they want. It allows users to search for a particular learning group or organization, a learning theme, a concept or incident; browse by category; compare concepts from different organizations; jump directly into the best summaries; or just wander through the collection.

Development of knowledge and learning resources

The programme encourages and supports learning groups to co-develop, produce, and share experience-based knowledge and resources on NRM. Small grants enable groups to develop appropriate and participatory ways to systematically document, organize, and package knowledge and lessons from their CBNRM experiences; share knowledge products and processes that reflect CBNRM principles in innovative ways and formats; maximize use and application of the learning resources by providing wider access to various CBNRM stakeholders; and promote collective ownership of the knowledge generated and shared.

Learning groups are encouraged to use indigenous communication formats, folk media, community media, and other formats or modes that can be used by development practitioners, as well as by primary stakeholders in their communities, and that can be shared regionally.

The current programme provided a venue for showcasing the learning groups' work at a "festival of CBNRM learning resources" during its final regional evaluation and planning workshop. Selected learning resources are being further developed as a multimedia package that can be adopted or adapted and used for a wider range of audiences in the countries participating in the ALL in CBNRM programme.

Improved distance learning platform

Improvements were also made to the distance-learning platform based on feedback from the participants in the Isang Bagsak and ALL in CBNRM programmes. ALL in CBNRM started with an electronic forum (e-forum) or discussion board as the primary mode of distance learning. During in-country team workshops and after the first theme discussion, programme mentors found that a considerable number of learners could not easily access the e-forum for two reasons – slow Internet connectivity or incompatibility of servers; and low levels of literacy or unfamiliarity with the Internet.

In trying to solve these problems, the programme's knowledge management team created an e-mail group that provided the postings to those who found it difficult to use the e-forum. More participants were able to read this information sent directly to their e-mail account. After implementation of the e-mail group, postings from individual participants increased; in Isang Bagsak, postings were primarily group syntheses.

Another improvement in the distance-learning platform was the expansion of a resource centre on the ALL in CBNRM website. Selected reference materials from the Isang Bagsak's compendium and links to useful websites were uploaded in that section of the website.

However, learning groups with good Internet connection, especially the Philippine groups, preferred the e-forum with its own website over the e-mail group, as the latter clogged their mail inboxes.

Changes in learning groups' capacities

The composition of the learning groups is quite fluid. Some are project teams within an organization, units of an organization, team leaders representing the units of an organization, or the organization itself. Others are made up of a loose network of people from various organizations or a multisectoral programme with members from different organizations. Still, others consist of a network of communities led by their various facilitators. The learning groups also vary in strength, familiarity with participatory approaches, and knowledge of the ecosystems they work in and the CBNRM issues they are focusing on.

The Isang Bagsak programme was composed of eight diverse learning groups representing – academe (3), government agencies

(3), and NGOs (2) in Cambodia, the Philippines, and Vietnam. On the other hand, the ALL in CBNRM learning groups are dominated by NGOs (6 out of 9), followed by academe (3); government agencies are represented in three multisectoral groups that have NGOs or an academic institution as the active partner. ALL in CBNRM has also spread to six Southeast Asian countries, adding Indonesia, Laos, and Thailand to the original three (Fig. 4).

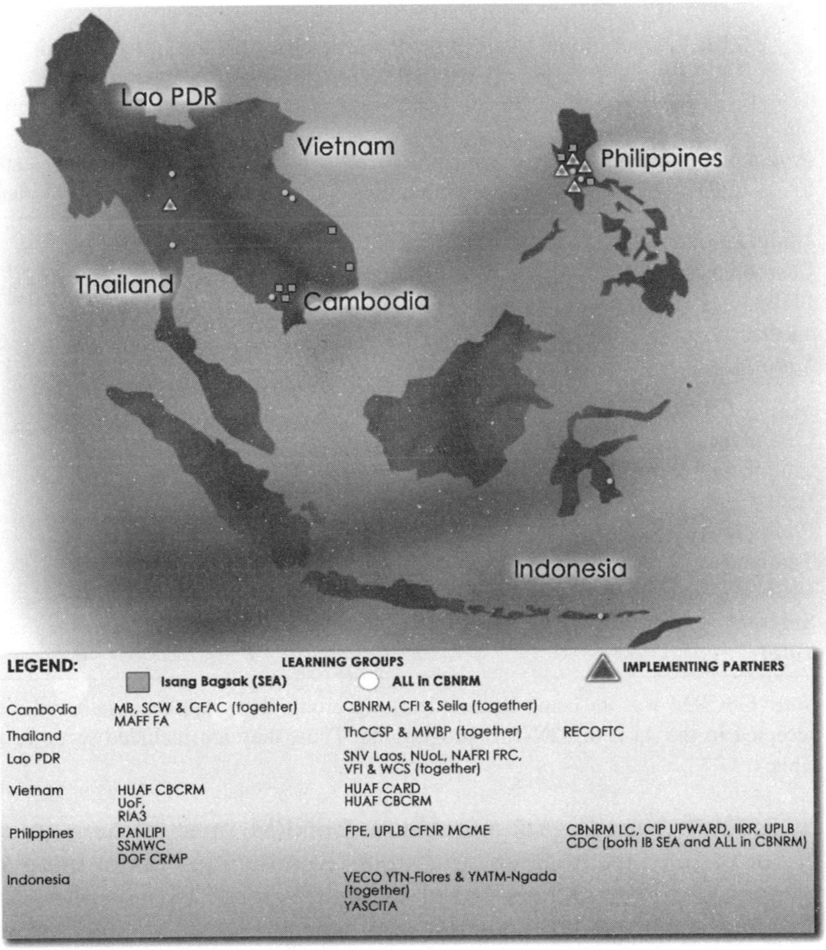

Fig. 4. Beginning with Isang Bagsak learning groups in Cambodia, the Philippines, and Vietnam, the ALL in CBNRM programme has spread to include Indonesia, Lao PDR, and Thailand.

Note: One organization does not necessarily correspond to one learning group. Some learning groups are composed of two or three affiliated organizations.

The operational focus of the learning groups can be classified into three types –

1. Projects working directly with specific local communities.
2. Issue- or discipline-specific programmes at the national or central level working with many local communities
3. National or central programmes for policymakers and service providers, such as extension workers, local government units, and teachers (Table 7).

Table 7. Operational focus of the learning groups in the Isang Bagsak and All in CBNRM programmes

Programme and country	Operational focus Specific local communities	 Many communities	 Policymakers and service providers
Isang Bagsak			
Cambodia	0	1	1
Philippines	1	1	1
Vietnam	3	0	0
Subtotal	4	2	2
ALL in CBNRM			
Cambodia	0	0	1
Indonesia	2	0	0
Laos	0	0	1
Philippines	1	0	1
Thailand	0	0	1
Vietnam	2	0	0
Subtotal	5	0	4
Total	**9**	**2**	**6**

Note: CBCRM was an Isang Bagsak learning group. They applied again and were accepted in the ALL in CBNRM programme. Thus, they are included twice in the table.

For both Isang Bagsak and ALL in CBNRM, most learning groups (9 out of 17) directly served grassroots communities. Six of these are composed of researchers based in a university, two were NGOs, and one was a government research agency.

1. Southern Sierra Madre Wildlife Center, Miriam College, Philippines.
2. Hue University of Agriculture and Forestry, Community-Based Coastal Resource Management Project, Vietnam (HUAF–CBCRM).
3. Research Institute for Aquaculture No. 3, Vietnam (RIA 3).
4. University of Fisheries, Vietnam (UoF).

5. Hue University of Agriculture and Forestry, Center for Agricultural Forestry Research and Development, Vietnam (HUAF–CARD).
6. Makiling Center for Mountain Ecosystems (MCME).
7. VECO Indonesia in partnership with Yayasan Tananua-Flores, Indonesia (VECO YTN-Flores).
8. Yayasan Cinta Alam, Indonesia (YASCITA).

Six of the 17 learning groups were centrally located and dealt with service providers or local government units or policymakers rather than local communities.

1. Cheyor Cambodia composed of members from Mlup Baitong, Save Cambodia's Wildlife, and the Community Forestry Alliance for Cambodia.
2. Department of Finance (DoF) Community-based Resource Management Project (CBRMP), Philippines, under Isang Bagsak SEA.
3. Team from CBNRM Learning Institute (CBNRM-LI), Community Forestry International (CFI), and Seila programme.
4. Team from SNV Laos, National University of Laos (NUOL), Forestry Research Center of the National Agriculture and Forestry Research Institute (NAFRI), Village Focus International (VFI) Laos, and Wildlife Conservation Society.
5. Foundation for the Philippine Environment (FPE).
6. Team from the Thailand Programme of the World Conservation Union (Th-IUCN; formerly Mekong Wetlands Biodiversity Conservation and Sustainable use Programme) and the Thailand Collaborative Country Support Programme (TCCSP) under ALL in CBNRM.

Only two learning groups, both belonging to the earlier Isang Bagsak programme, were central programmes serving many communities: Cambodia's Forestry Administration under its Ministry of Agriculture, Forestry and Fisheries, and the lawyers' NGO Tanggapang Panligal Ng Katutubong Pilipino (PANLIPI) in the Philippines.

In general, the learning groups work in two dominant areas – forests and upland ecosystems (9.5 of the 17); four others focus on marine and aquatic resources. Three groups work in both contexts, while one of the two organizations comprising one learning group works in wetland biodiversity (Table 8).

Table 8. Natural resource management contexts of the various learning groups

Programme and country	Upland ecosystems and forests	Marine and aquatic resources	Both forest and marine resources	Wetlands/ inland waters
Isang Bagsak				
Cambodia	2	0	0	0
Philippines	2	0	1	0
Vietnam	1	2	0	0
Subtotal	5	2	1	0
ALL in CBNRM				
Cambodia	0	0	1	0
Indonesia	1	1	0	0
Laos	1	0	0	0
Philippines	1	0	1	0
Thailand	0.5*	0	0	0.5*
Vietnam	1	1	0	0
Subtotal	4.5	2	2	0.5
Total	*9.5*	*4*	*3*	*0.5*

*One of the two organizations making up a learning group.

Part 2: Achievements and challenges

Toward a typology of adaptive learning and capacity for participatory approaches to CBNRM

To determine how the Isang Bagsak and ALL in CBNRM programmes are influencing mindsets and practices among CBNRM researchers and practitioners in Southeast Asia, an inventory of the entry capacities of the learning groups was made to compare with gains from involvement in the programmes. Learning gains were assessed from participants' narratives provided in the documentation from regional evaluation and planning workshops, in-team mentoring workshops, and, in the case of Isang Bagsak, from case stories of PDC experiences submitted by learning groups.

By examining entry capacities and learning gains, an attempt was made to discover whether there was a pattern or set of factors which could be used to interpret them. At the surface level, it was found that the entries were interpretated as per their own constructs. Freire's (1970, cited and discussed in Cadiz 2005) theories of dialogue, praxis, and conscientization were relied and built upon to do this.

Learning and capacity building span a continuum from primarily theoretical understanding to primarily practical application, where the midpoint is characterized by in-depth understanding emanating from good complementarity of theory and practice, i.e., praxis. Seven points can be distinguished on this continuum:

1. Primarily theoretical understanding (PT).
2. More theoretical understanding (MT).
3. Near praxis leaning toward theoretical understanding (NtPrx).
4. Praxis (Prx).
5. Near praxis leaning toward practical understanding (NpPrx).
6. More practical understanding (MP).
7. Primarily practical understanding (PP).

In scrutinizing the learning inventories, an easy fit of all the reported learning gains with the proposed typology was not found, i.e., categorizing adaptive capacities did not turn out to be simple.

"More theoretical" and "more practical" are, of course, gradations and both can be said to represent capacity development in process. The desired movement from entry capacity is toward the centre (4 on the above list). However, the reported learning gains did not follow this move toward praxis. Some merely implied additional practical or theoretical understanding, but no deepening. The various movements are represented in Fig. 5.

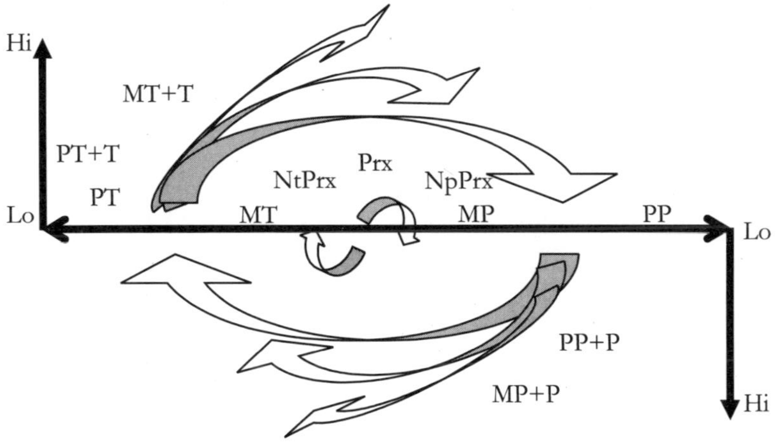

Fig. 5. A framework for evaluating adaptive learning of and capacity for participatory approaches to CBNRM

The sum of the envisioned adaptive learning/capacities is captured by a dynamic and expanding helix in Figure 4 (the portrayal of the ALL in CBNRM's learning modalities), i.e., an expanding cyclical process toward the centre of the theory-practice axis. It is together a meeting, a dance of practice and theory. Theory does not refer to knowledge detached from experience and action, but synthesized, abstracted, or generalised knowledge arrived at after reflection on CBNRM actions and experiences. Such reflection is also enriched by knowledge from outside a learning group's experience, such as those made explicit in the publications and postings of other learning groups in the region or of programme facilitators, resource persons, and other published or fugitive works they might cite in discussions.

Building this kind of capacity for participatory approaches to CBNRM is adaptive by definition. However, it does not happen overnight nor is it attainable by all groups. For example, some learning groups may have increased their knowledge and skills, but unless they bring this new expertise into the cycle of praxis, the change in their behaviour does not meet the goal of the programme.

Figure 6 shows how the profiles of the learning groups in the two programmes differed, in terms of their entry capacities. Six of nine groups in the current programme were relatively strong (near praxis) in capacity at the outset, compared with one such group in the earlier programme (praxis). The two arrows departing from Prx represent one organization, PANLIPI. PANLIPI (when they joined Isang Bagsak) was already high in praxis at the outset. They said

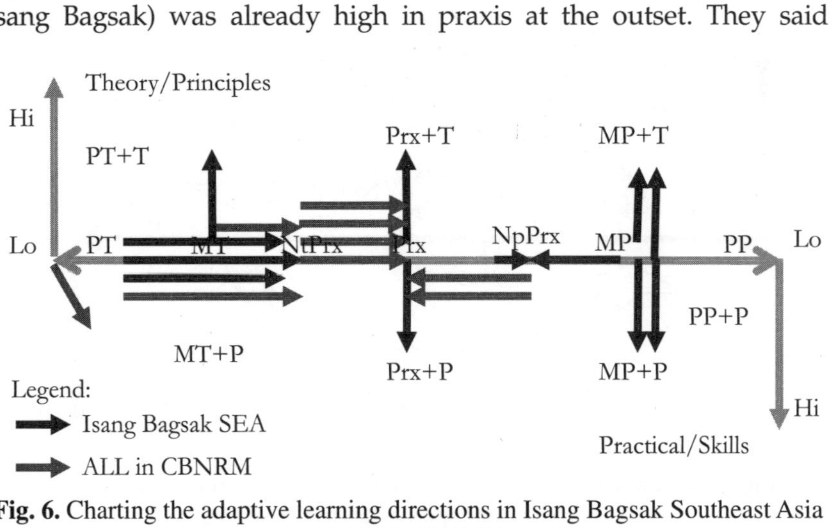

Fig. 6. Charting the adaptive learning directions in Isang Bagsak Southeast Asia and ALL in CBNRM.

they gained additional practical knowledge and deepened their members' perspectives in their participation in Isang Bagsak. Thus, they gained both in terms of increase in theoretical and practical knowledge. Likewise, only one group had low entry capacity at the outset of the ALL in CBNRM programme.

The learning gains of the ALL in CBNRM groups were of the more desired type, illustrated by horizontal movement toward the centre or praxis (Fig. 6). Six out of nine learning groups achieved deepened praxis by the end of the programme, while two also moved toward the centre to near praxis on the theoretical side. The progress of a good number of Isang Bagsak groups (four out of eight) (Table 9), on the other hand, illustrates mere addition of skills or knowledge or both (vertically) and not necessarily a move toward praxis that integrates theory or knowledge with practice or skills (horizontally toward the centre).

Table 9. Changes in capacity of learning groups in the Isang Bagsak and ALL in CBNRM programmes

Direction and level of adaptive learning	Isang Bagsak	ALL in CBNRM
Horizontal toward praxis	*3 groups*	*8 groups*
Near praxis leaning toward theoretical understanding ▶ praxis		HUAF–CARD HUAF–CBCRM MCME FPE
Near praxis leaning toward practical understanding ▶ praxis		VECO (with YTN-Flores and YMTM-Ngada) YASCITA
More practical ▶ near praxis leaning toward practical understanding	Cheyor Cambodia	
More theoretical ▶ near praxis leaning toward theoretical understanding		Cambodia (CBNRM-LI, CFI, Seila)
Primarily theoretical ▶ near praxis leaning toward theoretical understanding	HUAF–CBCRM UoF	Thailand (TCCSP and Th-IUCN)
Vertical toward increased knowledge and skills	4 groups	1 group
Increased practical knowhow	DoF-CRMP	Laos (NUOL, NAFRI, VFI)
Increased theoretical	MAFF	

Direction and level of adaptive learning	Isang Bagsak	ALL in CBNRM
understanding and practical knowhow	PANLIPI SSMWC	
Diagonal toward praxis with addition of knowledge and skills	*1 group*	*No groups*
Low theoretical understanding and practical knowhow ▶ near praxis leaning toward practical understanding	RIA 3	

Note: CBNRM Learning Institute (CBNRM-LI); Community Forestry International (CFI); Department of Fisheries; Coastal Resources Management Project (DoF-CRMP); Foundation for the Philippine Environment (FPE); Hue University of Agriculture and Forestry, Center for Agricultural Forestry Research (HUAF–CARD); Hue University of Agriculture and Forestry, Community-Based Coastal Resource Management project (HUAF–CBCRM); International Union for Conservation of Nature (IUCN); Ministry of Agriculture, Forestry and Fisheries (MAFF); Makiling Center for Mountain Ecosystems (MCME); National Agriculture and Forestry Research Institute (NAFRI); National University of Laos (NUOL); Tanggapang Panligal Ng Katutubong Pilipino (PANLIPI); Research Institute for Agriculture No. 3 (RIA 3); Southern Sierra Madre Wildlife Center (SSMWC); Thailand Collaborative Country Support Programme (TCCSP); Thailand Programme of the World Conservation Union (Th-IUCN); University of Fisheries (UoF); Village Focus International (VECO – VFI); Yayasan Tananua-Flores (YTN-Flores); Yayasan Mitra Tani Mandiri de Ngada (YMTM-Ngada); Yayasan Cinta Alam (YASCITA).

Three of the nine ALL in CBNRM learning groups comprise several organizations, making it difficult to pin down their individual gains in capacity for CBNRM. For example, the two organizations making up the Thai learning group appear to differ in their entry capacities.

As observed by Cadiz (2006), some groups demonstrated more dramatic learning gains than others during the Isang Bagsak programme. These were the groups who, at the start of the programme, had low or primarily theoretical entry capacities and ended up near praxis. All three Vietnamese learning groups demonstrated these outstanding learning gains.

HUAF–CBCRM and the UoF in Vietnam entered the Isang Bagsak programme with low primarily theoretical (PT) capacities for PDC. After completing the learning programme, these groups demonstrated improved capacities in implementing PDC approaches and tools in their CBNRM projects. HUAF–CBCRM, in particular, was able to apply PDC in planning, awareness building, capacity development, and monitoring and evaluation activities for the Tam Giang Lagoon development projects.

Most apparent among the Isang Bagsak participants' reported learning gains are their enhanced confidence and clearer and wider understanding of PDC processes in CBNRM, plus the added value of gaining new skills in PDC. For the ALL in CBNRM programme, what the learners valued most was the opportunity their participation provided to reflect on their experiences collectively within their learning groups. In this process, they were serendipitously building their own team spirit. A second layer of this collective reflection was the opportunity the programme gave them to share and learn from other groups in the region. The company and comradeship they shared with similar groups facing similar challenges and addressing the same goals encouraged them and reinforced their philosophy, theoretical knowledge, methods and practice of CBNRM.

Tracking adaptive capacity and learning in terms of improved livelihoods: the case of Isang Bagsak

The greatest challenge of the programme is to study how changes in capacity and learning might improve learning groups' accomplishments in working with communities and contributing to improved livelihoods and quality of life.

Four of the eight organizations participating in Isang Bagsak applied PDC at the community level to give local people control over conservation and judicious management of their natural resources. Through participatory appraisal, participatory planning, perseverance in dialoguing, and innovative communication approaches, the coastal resource management projects in central Vietnam raised local people's awareness and understanding of NRM problems affecting their livelihoods.

For example, increased understanding inspired local people working with the Research Institute for Aquaculture No. 3 (RIA 3) in Vietnam to make recommendations for lobster resource management – release lobster brood stocks offshore with contributions from local fishermen and the government; keep lobsters in cages until their eggs are hatched; tax both fishing and lobster culture; close the fishing season periodically; and tax lobster culturists and lobster seed fishermen for use of resources. The tax revenues would be used by government to fund conservation practices, such as the release of lobster brood stocks.

In addition, people in the two communes with their local leaders organized self-management teams to enforce proper waste management and care of aquatic resources. According to RIA 3, the number of people participating in self-management teams increased from 59 in 2004 to 83 in 2005. Over that period, participants increased the number of lobsters released offshore from 59 to 100 and took other steps toward the sound management of their coastal resources.

In the Philippines, indigenous communities were able to negotiate with local government to install a community water system and with the local waterworks office to waive its fees. They campaigned for and secured the support of the Department of Environment and Natural Resources in banning the use of chain saws in their forest and organized to carry out forest resource management plans. PDC opened the minds of another group of Filipino researchers to listen to, understand, and respond to the needs of their NRM community. They secured their institution's commitment to a volunteer literacy and numeracy programme to strengthen primary education in the community and help establish good relations in conjunction with initiatives to expand a watershed conservation project.

Two M.Sc. students in Vietnam approached the challenge of tracking adaptive learning and capacity in terms of improved rural livelihoods in a different way. Pham Tran (2007) used a conventional survey interview approach to analyse this issue at the individual level. She interviewed 27 researchers and practitioners in the HUAF–CARD learning group that participated in the Isang Bagsak pilot project. Dao Mong (2007) used Davies and Dart's (2005) "most significant change" technique to track changes in the capacities of another Vietnamese learning group in the next phase of the Isang Bagsak programme.

They analyzed researchers' capacity in participatory CBNRM approaches with the behaviourist view of knowledge, attitudes, and practice as domains of change in capacity. The former was more researcher-structured while the latter, more open-ended, giving leeway to the view of the researched.

In tracking researchers' capacity to work with rural communities, Pham Tran noted:

> The farmer respondents ... described the CBNRM researchers as enthusiastic, amiable, thoughtful, kind, and mindful of the farmers' welfare. The Hong Ha respondents also said that the researchers could communicate clearly and concretely, and that the farmers understood the researchers' instructions easily. The farmers further noted how the researchers mingled with them in the field and how many local farmers had the chance to get involved in the CBNRM project ... . Farmer respondents said that the CBNRM Project exemplified "words together with action," that is, researchers not only instructed or trained the farmers, but also worked in the field with them.

On the capacities of the researchers, Dao Mong found,

> In the project "Community-based management of spiny lobster culture areas in Xuan Dai Bay with participation of the local community," the RIA 3 team carried out PDC activities where they coordinated closely with the various stakeholders of the project, including the lobster culturists, hamlet leaders, commune authorities, and local residents. The activities spanned initial gathering of benchmark data about the two hamlets, to involving the stakeholders, down to the other PDC steps such as application of PDC tools to encourage community participation in project activities.
>
> The RIA 3 team applied interpersonal communication skills in a clever manner to reduce the gap between the local people and the project staff at the beginning of the project. The highlight of the project's PDC activities was a night of performance of traditional media comprising singing and amateur theatre at the field site in order to enhance local villagers' awareness of properly using their surrounding natural resources and in keeping these surroundings clean. The PDC activities carried out did not necessarily correspond to separate PDC steps as outlined by Bessette (2004), but more in an integrated, flexible fashion as he qualified.

In terms of influence on the community, Pham Tran reported that farmer respondents said the project helped to enhance farmers' knowledge of technologies and their capacities for livestock raising, cultivation, aquaculture, and the use of fertilizers and insecticides. It also improved farmers' livelihoods:

> A large proportion of the Hong Ha respondents (84.62%) considered their knowledge of scientific technology and their economic well-being more enhanced with their participation in the CBNRM project. They

> said they were freer and more self-confident to face groups and the CBNRM researchers. They no longer worried about food shortage.
>
> As a whole, they said their lives were better and more comfortable. Children could now go to school and they had enough food for all in the family. With some savings, some bought new furniture and means of transport. Their other observations included higher incomes, increased farm yields or animal production, and improved farming. They attributed the following changes to the CBNRM project: their enhanced knowledge on technologies; communication facilities, an irigation system and a humanity house; roads, bridges, schools, electricity, and other infrastructure.

They attributed not only their enhanced knowledge to the project, but also new communication facilities, an irrigation system, roads, bridges, schools, and electricity.

Dao Mong's account of changes in the NRM community also touched on quality of life, as well as on the enhanced capacities of villagers:

> One lady ... told of how her family's lobster production increased, enabling them to pay for the children's school fees and acquire family comforts like a television set, a motorcycle, a refrigerator, and a comfort room in their house. [Others]... told of their increased capacities, namely their enhanced awareness and knowledge plus improved practices on using and conserving lobster resources, maintenance of cleanliness in the environment of the lobster farm, and sharing of information with others.
>
> Specifically, the lobster culturists, local residents, and local authorities had become aware of the factors affecting their lobster culture efficiency, such as quality and size of lobster seed stocked into cages, culture technology or deteriorated water quality. The local people's MSC [Most Significant Change] stories also showed their realization of the importance of keeping their surrounding environment clean not just for lobster culture but for their health as well. Furthermore, beyond gaining knowledge from the project, the local people started sharing information with others in the community who were not directly part of the project. These findings suggest capacity enhancement as an important domain to study in MSC, as a prelude to achieving changes in people's quality of life.

The attitude of various stakeholders changed considerably during the project. As Dao Mong said, "Using PDC in the project implementation empowered various stakeholders in terms of participation, sharing, learning, and managing their natural resources."

In terms of the sustainability of local community organizations, Dao Mong noted that the establishment of self-management teams in two hamlets in central Vietnam (the NRM project sites) resulted in a remarkable change in the hamlets' organization. However, when the NRM project ended, the sustainability of the self-management teams became a concern. Left on their own, only a few members remained active in these teams at the time of her study. However, Dao Mong's visit to facilitate the community's selection of their most significant change stories spawned a meeting to revive the self-management teams, indicating the importance of periodic follow-up after a project terminates.

From improved knowledge and skills to development outcomes

After twenty months of sharing and learning together, the ALL in CBNRM learning groups showed a significant increase in their knowledge and understanding of the various participatory development approaches used in CBNRM. They also had a better appreciation of the similarities and differences among various CBNRM contexts in Southeast Asia. What is particularly interesting is that, in a short period, these changes in capacities are being translated into actions that foster more community participation, inclusion of more stakeholders, and changes in the policy environment.

Concrete development impacts may not necessarily be visible yet, as these require more time, but the energy being put into this programme and the innovations and new social spaces created by the learning groups and implementing partners are geared toward more sustainable, people-centred, and participatory CBNRM efforts in rural Southeast Asia.

Indonesia

There are two learning groups in Indonesia – VECO-Indonesia with two people's organizations (YTN-Flores and YMTM-Ngada) and YASCITA, an NGO that uses broadcast media in its development work. Both groups have increased their knowledge of participatory development approaches, especially in terms of stakeholder analysis, participatory monitoring and evaluation (PM & E), developing partnerships, and PDC.

Through ALL in CBNRM's small grants programme, VECO-Indonesia and YTN-Flores were able to develop a PM & E system for cacao marketing that incorporates new methods and tools into various participatory approaches. A new perspective on stakeholder relations and partnership influenced the planning and redesign of their development projects to involve local government and the church.

> "Before, they worked only with the communities in managing the land, not with government or the church or with other NGOs. An important change is that we learned to work with other stakeholders. After the introductory workshop, they started thinking about how to communicate with the government, the church, and the universities. Later on, there were many stakeholders talking about the same issue – how to minimize external inputs to sustainable agriculture."
>
> *Wrenges Widjoraras, VECO-Indonesia, ALL in CBNRM Evaluation and Planning Workshop Highlights, 8–10 January, 2008*

YASCITA members were able to apply their knowledge about participatory communication strategies in their media work by adopting a more multistakeholder approach. The organization also developed communication and mobilization strategies specific to their target media audience.

> "Before ALL in CBNRM, frankly, every strategy we did was by trial and error. We did not really have a systematic way of learning. By joining this programme, every goal is done by a specific step. Before the mentoring visit, we did not have a specific desk in our radio. We broadcast on every issue to the community. Now, we just focus on three main issues: environment, policy, and public service. With this, YASCITA can get more information and data that can be used for advocacy."
>
> *Muh. Aswan Zanynu, YASCITA, ALL in CBNRM Evaluation and Planning Workshop Highlights, 8–10 January, 2008*

Lao PDR

The Lao learning group consists of researchers from three independent organizations: the National Agriculture and Forestry Research Institute (NAFRI), the National University of Laos, and Village Focus International. They explained how experiences shared by VECO-Indonesia through e-forum discussion have influenced their monitoring and evaluation system.

> "We are impressed with the PM & E strategy used by VECO-Indonesia. We adopted it for our Marketing Analysis and Development for Non-timber Forest Products. Villagers, project officers, and consultants are all involved in identifying and measuring indicators. The PM & E process helps villagers understand the whole process and realize the stage of marketing development. It also encouraged local people to take more ownership of their actions."
>
> *Souvanhpheng Phommasane, NAFRI, ALL in CBNRM Evaluation and Planning Workshop Highlights, 8–10 January, 2008*

Besides sharing positive stories, they also shared some difficulties that they encountered in their participation in ALL in CBNRM. The Lao group started with 17 participants, but 19 months later, only seven remained active. Mr Souvanhpheng explained that many of his colleagues had no time to participate in the programme because of heavy workload and lack of concrete incentives. He particularly mentioned scholarships and accreditation in the university as examples of incentives that would induce his teammates to participate more actively.

Cambodia

The Cambodian group is composed of practitioners from three independent organizations working on the same cause – community forestry – Community Forestry International (CFI), CBNRM-LI, and the Seila programme. This group has gained considerable skill in developing partnerships. Previously, they simply provided funds or grants to their partner NGOs. However, after acquiring new knowledge and perspectives on partnerships, they established more meaningful relations with their partner organizations by offering technical support and capacity development activities.

The Cambodian group described how new partnerships led to skills training in the communities. Communities are now using self-evaluation tools in their CBNRM projects.

Like the Lao learning group, the Cambodian group also experienced difficulties in participating in ALL in CBNRM. Only 4 of the original 17 members remained active during the evaluation and planning workshop. Mr Long Sona explained that many of his teammates moved to other organizations. They also had heavy workloads that prevented them from participating actively.

Philippines

The two learning groups in the Philippines were the Foundation for the Philippine Environment (FPE), a grant-making NGO with 20 project sites throughout the country; and the Makiling Center for Mountain Ecosystems (MCME), a research and development centre at the UPLB College of Forestry and Natural Resources. It is responsible for managing and protecting the Mt. Makiling Forest Reserve, which forms part of the University's territory.

In 2006, it was timely for MCME to participate in ALL in CBNRM, as its participatory upland project in the Dampalit Watershed had just started. Lessons on how to approach the community and set goals and objectives were applied in its planning activities with partner communities. Devolving decision-making power to the communities has made them more confident and competent in comanaging the upland project. Community leaders now serve as resource people when students and foreign researchers visit the study site. ALL in CBNRM also gave MCME an opportunity to further strengthen its participatory practices in the field through a research grant. The MCME team produced a video in which the scriptwriters and actors were community members. Women farmers likewise involved themselves in income-generating activities as well as in the production of the video.

In contrast with MCME, FPE was involved in a number of CBNRM projects at various stages when they entered ALL in CBNRM. It was also undergoing organization-wide evaluation that led to a shift in its perspective and CBNRM framework and approaches.

Technical field backstopping of multistakeholder processes and PM & E significantly influenced FPE's CBNRM work. New knowledge about multistakeholder processes was incorporated into the design and implementation of its community-based forest corridor development project in the southern part of the Philippines. This has led to inclusion of more stakeholders and better coordination with partner organizations. New perspectives on PM & E also helped FPE review its existing monitoring and evaluation system. It is now planning to incorporate new practices into its frameworks and operations.

Both FPE and MCME recognized that ALL in CBNRM facilitated a more systematic and structured learning process for their organizations and provided opportunities for their staff to work more effectively as a team.

They cited some problems associated with the participatory way of working with the communities and partner organizations. For example, MCME feared that too much interaction with their partner communities would result in dependence of these communities on them. FPE, on the other hand, noted its tendency to work directly with people's organizations, overlooking the role of partner NGOs as the intermediate and direct link between FPE and communities.

Vietnam

The Vietnam Learning Group comprised two teams from HUAF – the Upland Project of CARD and CBCRM Project.

At the community level, the CARD group had an interesting story about a recent project to build a community house. They showed that a participatory approach was much more successful than previous methods of entering a community with their own preconceived plan. Despite a lack of funds, the community successfully built its own house, which it had identified as a primary need. The community provided most of the resources and manpower from within the village.

Le Quang Minh, a member of HUAF–CARD, explained how participatory approaches improved the livelihoods of minority groups living in the community described by Pham Tran above:

> "Hong Ha is one of the mountainous communes in Thua Thien Hue province, with five ethnic groups namely: Co Tu, Paco, Pahy, Ta oi, and few "kinh" people from the lowland, who came to settle there. In 1998, the CBNRM project was implemented in Hong Ha commune. Many local people are too shy to speak out in public, especially when they work with a research group from the university. The poor, especially the women, usually feel too inferior to participate in the discussion.

In identifying with the Hong Ha people their priority needs, we have attempted to use simple and available materials for making illustrations, such as stones, corn kernels, and nuts. Applying PDC tools flexibly has created significant change among the researchers in that they were encouraged to exercise their creativity. In carrying out project activities, the research team also trained the people on how to use fertilizer, how to arrange fruit trees in the garden, and how to prepare the pond and lake before breeding young fish.

The most significant change is that such training conducted in the field has played an important role in transferring science-based practices to the local people. This has remarkably improved the productivity of crops and livestock. The local people's livelihood has improved; which in turn helped to reduce pressure on the natural resources."

Le Quang Minh, HUAF–CARD, Video footage of interview during Field Mentoring Visit, 27 November – 3 December, 2007.

The CBCRM group shared a story about how learning gains from ALL in CBNRM helped them convince local government officials to accept and support community-based projects.

"The greatest challenge we encountered was opposition from local government officials. They did not agree with our approach on participatory planning. With some experience in participatory development communication, we tried to conduct many communication activities, like workshops, so that commune officials will believe that our approach is effective for resource management. It took us one year before they agreed to cooperate with us to apply participatory planning in the commune. Through this story, you can see that the communication is very important in convincing the government officials about the new approach, which is very different from the traditional approach."

Truong Quang Hoang, CBCRM Project, Video footage of interview during Field Mentoring Visit, 27 November – 3 December, 2007.

Thailand

The Thailand learning group is composed of practitioners and researchers from two organizations – Thailand Country Collaborative Support Programme and the Thailand Programme of The World

Conservation Union (formerly Mekong Wetland Biodiversity Conservation Programme). This group recognized that ALL in CBNRM has structured their internal and organizational learning. It facilitated a more open attitude toward knowledge sharing and mentoring between young employees and senior staff. The group also produced a CD of songs for young people containing some of the lessons they had learned through e-forum discussions. In addition, they translated into Thai and featured the theme "Developing partnerships" in their newsletter, which is distributed among their partner organizations.

How learning took place

In this section, an attempt is made to explain how learning took place among the Isang Bagsak and ALL in CBNRM learning groups. Some groups are chosen as "good" examples on the basis of the advancement in their capacity from their entry level toward praxis. To arrive at some plausible explanations of how adaptive learning took place in ALL in CBNRM, there was an attempt to identify the strengths and weaknesses of each learning modality based on the experience of the learning groups and describe the quality of their participation and interaction. An attempt was also made to identify some contextual factors (political, cultural, and organizational) that influenced the learning processes during both Isang Bagsak and ALL in CBNRM programmes.

Face-to-face discussions

Overall, face-to-face discussions fostered learning through teamwork and systematic organizational learning. They gave each learning group an opportunity to sit together and discuss CBNRM in a more systematic manner, and most learning groups appreciated how these discussions structured their internal organizational learning. VECO-Indonesia, for example, discussed the thematic areas of CBNRM with its partner organizations, YTN-Flores and YMTM-Ngada. It also facilitated cross-learning among its partner organizations and helped strengthen existing linkages. FPE, on the other hand, involved non-programme, primarily administrative staff in its face-to-face team discussions. This practice benefited FPE by making these staff more confident and competent in their work.

Some learning groups, MCME in particular, held separate meetings for ALL in CBNRM, whereas others included ALL in CBNRM in the agenda for their regular team and executive committee meetings. At times, when meeting face-to-face was impossible, some learning groups explored new ways of collaboration, such as the use of mobile phones, email and Internet-relay chat.

In terms of quality of participation and interaction, face-to-face team discussions became a good venue for sharing individual learning experiences, mistakes, and lessons learned during the CBNRM process. Some learning groups, particularly the Cambodian group, claimed that ALL in CBNRM gave them opportunity to talk about matters they had never discussed earlier with their teammates.

Although face-to-face discussions were preferred by the learning groups, they had disadvantages – difficulty finding a time when everyone was available, internal politics that hindered some from participating meaningfully, and lack of financial support for those who had to travel to attend team meetings.

Regional workshops

In a network such as ALL in CBNRM, face-to-face interactions are essential to establish social relations with co-learners. They not only allow members to put "faces" to the names, but also instill a "heart" into CBNRM work, as the learners find motivation and inspiration from their colleagues in other countries who are doing similar work and are struggling with similar CBNRM issues and problems.

Regional workshops were designed so that they become avenues for cross-country learning rather than simply an evaluation activity. Both mid-term and final evaluation workshops enabled the learning groups to share how they practiced participatory development approaches in their various countries and project sites. They provided opportunities to build links and explore areas for future collaboration as well as giving participants a chance to meet resource persons and experts in the field.

What has not yet been achieved is a nuanced elaboration of partners' learning experiences with participatory-oriented research. ALL in CBNRM experimented with storytelling techniques to draw out field-based and lived experiences of the learning groups. However, it was apparent that many groups were unclear about what a "story" was and, thus, many responses lacked clear examples to back up described "changes." Most groups simply shared information.

Participants said the questions provided by the programme evaluation researchers, prevented them from telling their stories in a spontaneous manner. Speaking in English also contributed to the lack of concrete examples and detail in the stories. More reflection seems warranted on how best to use this method.

Field mentoring and technical backstopping

These supportive measures were intended to provide relevant technical assistance or advice pertaining to problems and issues in adopting participatory development approaches in the field and in improving the adaptive learning capacities of the learning groups and the communities they worked with.

The learning groups ranked this strategy highest in terms of its contribution to their learning. The interpersonal nature of the learning process between the mentors and the learning groups allowed immediate feedback and meaningful participation and interaction, not only by the learning groups, but also by other local stakeholders who were able to join the mentoring activities.

Field visits also helped the mentor organizations understand in greater depth the CBNRM issues and specific capacity building and mentoring needs of the learning groups they were guiding. This, in turn, enabled them to provide the necessary mentoring immediately (e.g., by holding a multistakeholder analysis workshop for FPE and advise on CBNRM policy research proposal preparation for MCME) and plan for future mentoring activities for both groups.

Regional online discussions

Online discussions enabled the learning groups from across Southeast Asia to share and exchange knowledge and experiences. It provided an opportunity to understand the diversity of CBNRM contexts, principles, and practices in Southeast Asia without the costs associated with travel to face-to-face meetings. Web-based forums and email groups also allowed automatic documentation of all discussions, which the learning groups could access and read at their convenience.

The learning groups also appreciated the input from resource people and online facilitators who helped them analyse their situations and issues. The resource people were from various disciplines, and introduced new ways of looking at CBNRM issues. They also provided relevant reference materials for further reading.

However, although the learning groups recognized the potential of regional online discussion as a fast and cost-efficient tool for disseminating information, this method of communication was also associated with problems of poor connectivity, language barriers, and low Internet literacy. Because of these difficulties, they ranked regional online discussions as the least preferred learning modality.

UPLB CDC's ongoing thematic and textual analyses of the online discussions has shown that most of the exchanges occurred between facilitator and learning group, with limited interaction between and among the learning groups. Furthermore, the quality and depth of the postings varied across the learning groups.

Contextual factors contributing to learning

Five factors explain the extent and quality of learning by participants in the Isang Bagsak and ALL in CBNRM programmes – commitment of the participants' institutions and supervisors to supporting their participation in the programme; emergence of local and regional networks of CBNRM learners; comparison of CBNRM knowledge with that of other participants; meeting fellow learners face-to-face; and the participatory tone of the learning process.

Institutional commitment

Efforts to evaluate ALL in CBNRM revealed that the learning groups who achieved praxis were those who were able to involve their managers, directors, and project leaders in the learning processes. For example, VECO-Indonesia's country representative was a member of the ALL in CBNRM mailing list and received theme discussion postings and updates about the programme. ALL in CBNRM activities carried out by the VECO learning group were also tied to their own project activities; the group's action research constituted one of the components of VECO-Indonesia's participatory monitoring and evaluation system. Moreover, VECO assigned a person to coordinate with its partner organizations and with the ALL in CBNRM secretariat. To a great extent, it solved the language problem of VECO participants and made coordination between VECO and the ALL in CBNRM programme management efficient.

Local and regional networks

In the programme, knowledge flowed back and forth between local and regional networks. Three of the nine learning groups were conglomerates of various CBNRM organizations; three were conglomerates of research and instruction units of universities; and one learning group was a conglomerate of people's organizations.

Efforts to monitor learning processes within the learning groups and their various CBNRM communities revealed that, in a few selected cases, local or community-based learning networks had formed. These were not necessarily obvious in the regional network e-forums. The Foundation for the Philippine Environment, for example, was able to pass on what its group learned from its technical backstopping field visits to its partner organizations in various parts of the Philippines. The knowledge gained in stakeholder analysis has influenced the planning activities and proposal development of the foundation's partner organizations, paving the way for the inclusion of wider range of CBNRM stakeholders at its project sites.

The reach of both the Isang Bagsak and the ALL in CBNRM programmes to the level of local communities, including farmers, fisher folk, women, and children, is yet to be tracked systematically.

Knowledge interfaces

Putting local knowledge into perspective by exposing to outside knowledge encourages innovation and adaptation. The Makiling Center for Mountain Ecosystems and the Cambodian learning group claimed that they appreciated the similarities between their CBNRM work and that of other learning groups, while others focused on the differences. Sharing of information helped participants understand that other CBNRM organizations in Southeast Asia experience the same problems they face. They appreciated hearing how other organizations have solved these problems. This new awareness broadened their understanding and often gave them a new perspective on their own situation.

YASCITA of Indonesia claimed that it gained relevant insights from similar cases or experiences in other countries with different governance systems. Its representatives pointed out that active sharing of experiences among the learning groups was one of the factors that contributed to learning.

Putting a face to the name

During the mid-term workshop, learning groups were able to meet their co-learners face-to-face. This enabled them to "put faces to the names" and in the process, they gained new friends.

After this workshop, the number of e-forum postings increased and learning groups became more open in their communication with the theme facilitators and co-learners. For instance, they were now able to confess that they did not understand some questions or that they were too busy to post their answers, enabling them to negotiate the schedule for regional theme discussions.

The participatory learning process

Learning took place horizontally or laterally (among CBNRM researchers and practitioners) and vertically (institutional policymaking to partner communities) through acknowledgement of the opinions, experiences, and views of a wide array of social actors at various levels. The participatory approach also enabled the integration of local and outside knowledge. Theme facilitators, resource people, and mentors were able to provide inputs to learning groups' experiences by bringing in their expertise on various aspects of CBNRM.

Conclusions: lessons and recommendations

Facilitating adaptive learning as social learning

As a social and adaptive learning process in itself, the Isang Bagsak and the ALL in CBNRM programmes have gained insight into how to run this kind of programme better, and this knowledge has helped them evolve.

First, the hierarchy of roles is changing. At times during the e-forum, regional workshop, and field mentoring visits, mentors have felt that they were the learners. Perhaps this means that the adaptive learning process also promotes equality.

Second, the experience highlighted the importance of face-to-face meetings and establishing relationships among co-learners and implementing partners. Learning might have been faster or more pronounced during the first part of the programme if the introductory face-to-face workshop had been regional rather than in-country or in-team meetings.

Third, the goal of Isang Bagsak and ALL in CBNRM was to enhance the capacities of the learning groups through sharing experiences and learning, both within the learning group and at the regional level. However, experience revealed that much of the adaptive learning process happened at the learning group level. The small grants programme and the field mentoring component of ALL in CBNRM are potential avenues for richer adaptive learning on participatory CBNRM approaches. Cross-visits between learning groups with a similar CBNRM context and problems are also worth exploring in future phases of the programme. As each learning group is unique in terms of structure and composition, the learning process may vary considerably from one group to another.

Finally, the programme must further study how to facilitate adaptive learning at the regional level. In addition to learning from in-country team discussions and sharing this knowledge with other learners at regional forums, learning groups need more opportunities to discuss with their co-learners how to adopt lessons creatively and intelligently and adapt them to local perspectives and situations.

Understanding adaptive learning

The exercise of reading and analyzing the narratives led to a conceptualization of how adaptive capacity development may be tracked. The narratives, which included postings by the learning groups in the regional e-forum and the project reports they wrote and submitted to their funders and organizations, may be read and analyzed in various ways.

For the purpose of applying further what we now call the adaptive learning evaluation framework or typology (Fig. 5), additional participatory monitoring and evaluation methods are recommended. Davies and Dart's (2005) "most significant change" techniques may provide a useful complementary approach to data gathering, although Dao Mong (2007) has pointed out difficulties in applying the technique in toto. Saludadez (2004) used the analysis of narratives, which she called "narratology," to analyze stories that people tell, using theories and tools drawn from language studies. The stories of forestry researchers' collaboration that she analyzed do not differ much from Davies and Dart's most significant change stories, except for the latter's focus on "significant changes."

Building on these methods, a process of open-ended self-assessment, in a tone of storytelling, is recommended at the learning group and partner mentors levels. But storytelling should be anchored in the adaptive learning framework, where the suggested typology may be used as a guide to locate where exactly in the map or framework the learning group finds itself.

Quantification, mainly as an aid to locating a learning group's adaptive learning capacity within the framework, is also possible. Adapted from Kelly's (1955) repertory grid technique for personal construct analysis, this requires filling in a matrix using the seven-point scale of the proposed adaptive learning typology. Recorded are the learning group's specific competencies as emphasized by the programme and the learning group's assessment of the levels of their competencies. Using multidimensional scaling, a group's adaptive learning capacity in participatory CBNRM approaches may then be located within the proposed framework. Further development, testing, simulation, and refinement of this evaluation framework and approach are recommended.

The agenda for further evaluating and investigating capacity development in Isang Bagsak and ALL in CBNRM remain an open arena. The programme has grown and become more complex, while remaining true to its design. A great challenge that this complexity poses is that of continuously making sense of how the programme translates adaptive learning and capacity development in participatory CBNRM approaches into reality.

Development communication as organizing

From a disciplinary view of development communication, the ALL in CBNRM programme is an excellent demonstration of communication in action, i.e., in its organizing role (Cooren and Taylor et al. 2006) and as constitutive (Craig 1999; Saludadez 2004) of the very processes of CBNRM in particular, and of sustainable development in general (Cadiz 2006).

As one programme partner asserted during the ALL in CBNRM programme orientation (before this name was adopted), the partnership of five organizations collaborating as mentors and programme implementers toward a centre of excellence in CBNRM in Southeast Asia is in itself an interesting action study. The programme becomes a programme through the collective efforts to serve rural communities and their natural resources. The loop goes even further than this, and it would be interesting to assess how the learning processes influence local and national policy.

Finally, writing this chapter has also been an adaptive learning process. The work has taken on a final form that is different from what its authors imagined. It became an exercise in analyzing narratives from ALL in CBNRM documentation, an act of striving to understand the programme, the groups involved in it, and the outcomes. A framework for evaluating adaptive learning and capacities in participatory CBNRM approaches was found in the process of interpreting and analyzing the learning and changes in capacity of its participants in the last two phases. This article has thus also demonstrated how communication is creative (Jean A. Saludadez, Assistant Professor and Director, Office of Academic Support and Instructional Services, University of the Philippines Open University, 2nd semester 2003–2004 while team teaching advanced communication theory and qualitative communication research courses, personal communication) in an adaptive fashion.

Learning in and from the field (Guizhou province, China).
Photo: Ronnie Vernooy.

4

Mainstreaming CBNRM in Chinese Higher Education

Zhang Li, Qi Gubo, and Ronnie Vernooy, with Long Zhipu and Jingsong Li

This case study focuses on participatory action learning in the country's higher education system. In Part 1, the background and the main elements of the capacity development initiative are described and, in Part 2, a summary of the learning outcomes at various levels is given and some reflections on the achievements till date are included. It draws on theory, on personal and active experience in the initiative, and on the findings of multiple participatory monitoring and evaluation (PM & E) activities carried out throughout the capacity development process. As part of the learning experimentation personal learning stories are included in this case study. These stories aim to give some insight in the everyday learning process that was experienced, among others, about the enrolment in the initiative, the linkages established, and the emergent features that have come about in the innovation process.

Part 1: The capacity development initiative

Challenges in China's higher education

The field visit experience described above is the key part of a new course at the College of Humanities and Development (COHD) at China Agricultural University (CAU) in Beijing: "Community-based natural resource management – an introduction." The course development experience – from design, through delivery, to

> "In interactions with local farmers of Guangxi province, I felt the importance of 'participatory development' and paid more attention to the role of local farmers in the elimination of poverty. In the past, I thought a good policy carried out by qualified officials would be enough to change everything evil into good, without any consideration of the participation of the poor and their feelings. But reality proves that way of thinking is wrong, because most government policies are not welcomed and may even be rejected by the farmers. On the contrary, farmers want to express their own demands and explore their resources – human, natural, and social resources. Thus, they show more enthusiasm and take more initiative for this communication and participation."
>
> *M.Sc. student, COHD, Beijing, March 2006*

evaluation – is part of a larger action research and capacity development initiative entitled "Participatory learning, curriculum development and mainstreaming of community-based natural resource management approaches in higher education in China" (COHD 2004). This initiative aims to contribute to the development and implementation of innovative, community-based and participatory development approaches in rural China.

The design and delivery of a CBNRM curriculum will train a new generation of rural development professionals. In a rapidly changing China, these professionals require more comprehensive knowledge and skills and stronger connections to rural realities, which are characterized by persistent poverty, a rapidly widening gap between poor and rich regions, increasing natural resource degradation, and widespread pollution (Hanson and Martin 2006).

However, it is not easy to bring about change in the country's large and still very hierarchical and bureaucratic higher education system. Although these days, there is much discourse about "reform," in practice, changes have been slow. Theoretical knowledge continues to be seen as the most valuable expression of science. There is little or no interest in addressing the practical problems that rural people face. Direct links and meaningful interactions between rural communities and staff and students remain rare (Li Xiaoyun and Li Ou 2003). Few students have a chance to do prolonged or in-depth fieldwork. People-centred approaches and systematic attention to the social and political dynamics of rural development are still not common in the agricultural and environmental sciences. "Hard" science approaches and a focus on technologies prevail.

Conventional lecturing remains the dominant method for instructing students. Students look up to the teachers, maintaining considerable distance – literally and figuratively. In classrooms, there is little room for critical reflection on the meaning, reasons, and methods of learning. Very few students have a chance to work as assistant teachers or researchers, and even fewer to do fieldwork that they organize and manage themselves. Most learning assignments are individual, and few opportunities exist to engage in and learn about teamwork.

The current minister of education, Zhou Ji, believes that "old" disciplines are due for review and new academic specialities should be established, based on China's socioeconomic development needs (Zhou Ji 2006). To create new specialities, a number of elements are needed – a clear description of the content matter (general level as well as course level), a feasible education plan, a sufficient number of qualified teachers, adequate materials and equipment, and funds. The minister provides the following guidelines for curriculum change – increase general knowledge; increase the number of elective courses; emphasize practical, experimental, and social interaction in courses; adopt a cross-disciplinary perspective; use creativity; and stimulate research as part of teaching and training.

Some efforts are being made to change the situation. In 1999, a small group of Chinese agricultural and rural development professionals initiated the Farmer-Centred Research Network (FCRN) to promote farmer-focused research and development at the national level by introducing participatory and CBNRM action research and teaching. The FCRN brings together staff from about 20 organizations, including agricultural academies (Institute of Plant Nutrient and Analysis, Inner-Mongolia Academy of Agricultural Sciences; Integrated Rural Development Research Centre, Guizhou Academy of Agricultural Sciences), universities (CAU, Jilin Agricultural University [JLAU], and the South-west Agricultural University), research centres (Centre for Chinese Agricultural Policy), and NGOs (the Ningxia Centre for Environmental Protection and Poverty Alleviation [HOPE] and the Centre for Biodiversity and Indigenous Knowledge, Kunming, Yunnan).

With support from COHD staff, the FCRN has gone through a first phase of capacity building and learning about this new approach. The second phase, which started in 2004, is strengthening and expanding on these achievements. The ultimate goal is to move the agricultural research and education system toward participatory, farmer-centred learning and action (Qi Gubo et al. 2005). In addition to carrying out participatory field research supported by targeted training activities, the network members are now realizing that it is essential to find ways to institutionalize these methods in China's higher education system.

Unfortunately, it appears to be more difficult to integrate participatory learning and action into the university curriculum than into some development agencies, perhaps because of the still very hierarchical nature of the higher education system and the strong resistance to change. Increasingly, this is creating a discontinuity between knowledge generation (in the classroom) and utilization (in the field), as higher education fails to keep pace with the increasingly serious problems of natural resource degradation and widespread rural poverty.

Innovative curriculum development is one key means to deal with this bottleneck, as it allows the introduction of a new, more relevant approach to learning to the new generation of development professionals. If new curricula and programmes can be introduced into the over 100 agricultural and related higher education institutions in China, more appropriate knowledge and skills could be generated and used. As one of the leading institutions for rural development study and learning in the higher education system in China, COHD has the responsibility of advising other universities about curriculum and programme development. This provides an opportunity for change and for a potentially large-scale application of the new approach that is aimed to develop and tried out in the coming years.

Within COHD, our work is housed in the Rural Development and Management (RDM) programme. Currently, this programme includes undergraduate, graduate, and Ph.D. levels. Several development themes are addressed in the key courses and related research undertaken across China. For example, research interests include poverty alleviation, development policies, community-based resource management, community/village governance, rural technology innovation, technology policies, development communication, participatory community development planning, gender and development, rural extension, human resource management, and children's participation in development. As of 2008, 28 teachers and faculty members were involved in research and teaching; they were responsible for about 250 undergraduates, 50 graduates (under RDM, regional economics, and sociology), and 80 Ph.D. candidates, who are shared with about six professors in other departments. All staff members have pursued development studies abroad; many of them are also consultants in rural development issues in China.

An exciting journey of exploration in CBNRM mainstreaming

by Qi Gubo, COHD, Beijing

Several of our graduated students who are now working in research institutes and development NGOs all over the country, sent me greetings again on New Year's day 2007. Their greetings brought back beautiful memories of time spent together. When I go back in time, I see thousands of e-mails and a great number of photos in front of me. They remind me of the long walk on road full of smiles, tears, confusion, day and night debates, endless talking, and, most important, happiness. These are the background images of the CBNRM mainstreaming process that we have gone through so far.

I don't remember exactly why, when, where, and how I joined this incredible journey. In the middle of 1998, when I moved to the College of Rural Development from the College of Economics and Management, getting involved in research based on a participatory approach was completely new to me. I was very excited. Encouraged by colleagues and supported by strong group work, I began to stay with farmers for longer periods of time. This introduced me to a different world of research. I learned rural development methods from my colleagues in the field, e.g., how to do project appraisal, planning, monitoring, and evaluation. I also started understanding concepts, such as farmers' perspectives, diversity, gender and development. After about two years of working and a half-year of additional training, I was lucky to become the coordinator of the Farmer-Centred Research Network. I was now fully captured by this magic journey, which showed me a novel way forward.

The most important thing for me was that I was working not only with good colleagues in my institute, but also with colleagues in other institutes who already realized that innovation and reform were needed. They worked hard toward more common understanding, joint research efforts, and collective action. Harmony and a happy mood are the principles and goals of my work and daily life, and so I was very lucky to have the chance to work with people who had the same objectives. This helped me delve deeper into participatory research and learning, and to capture the meaning of empowerment and the philosophy behind "putting the last first" or "beyond farmer first".

I understood more about "empowerment" in 1999 during a visit to the Guizhou Academy of Agricultural Sciences (GAAS). This was when I started to learn more about how to mobilize existing resources (ideas, knowledge, and skills) for the FCRN networking efforts supported by IDRC. IDRC's supervision facilitated the task of clarifying the roles and responsibilities of the various stakeholders involved in the network. As coordinator of the FCRN, which means working with about 20 academies, universities and NGOs in rural development or agricultural technology, I learned how to pay attention to partners' needs and interests, to design appropriate modalities of activities according to different situations, and to coordinate my multiple and sometimes conflicting roles of coordinator, teacher, and researcher. I also learned how to work in a multidisciplinary team. I learned during the process of providing support to the network partners and in the process of communicating with colleagues from our own college and from other institutes.

Becoming miracle agents

One conversation in June 2004 led me to move into a more exciting phase of my journey. Ronnie Vernooy (from IDRC), Li Xiaoyun (the dean of COHD), and I, sat around a dinner table without much interest in the food set in front of us. We only talked ... . The idea of "centres of CBNRM excellence" was introduced by Ronnie, and Xiaoyun had responded in a very supportive way. Xiaoyun then presented his ideas for a "participatory learning and CBNRM mainstreaming in Chinese higher education" initiative. The three of us thought that this idea would fit very well with the centres of excellence picture. Based on my observations of students' learning practices, I felt that the ideas tabled that evening were very promising. Although our students did a lot of fieldwork, most of them did so without continuity and integration with their thesis research. At the same time, although we delivered courses on development theories, development methods, and some specific development topics, the students' feedback indicated that they did not really understand what exactly our Rural Development and Management (RDM) education programme is pursuing.

I also thought that these new ideas were relevant to the many debates raging at that moment, in particular the one concerning conventional academic research versus field-based and action-oriented studies.

However, I was not very clear about how the new ideas would be put into practice. I thought that a participatory curriculum development approach, which informed both the centres of excellence plan and Xiaoyun's CBNRM mainstreaming idea, was just a kind of participatory teaching method.

At first, I did not pay much attention to the development of Xiaoyun's ideas into a full research proposal. But I became more interested when, during exchanges of emails between Xiaoyun and Ronnie about the proposal, the picture of combining existing CBNRM efforts in Guizhou and Guangxi in China and other regions in Asia with the education programme in RDM became clearer. This was a very new and radical proposition – to build up a solid practice stage for the next generation of RDM students *during* their study period and to build strong bridges to partner institutes with a focus on CBNRM and participatory development approaches, allowing for a two-way stream of people and experiences. Although there are many students, graduated from our RDM programme, who are now working for NGOs, and some as volunteers in partner institutes (with high spirit and strength), no systematic and strong linkages exist between our programme and rural practice oriented organizations.

Change will be brought about by the young, dynamic, bright and *brave* people, in the same way as the pioneers of a CBNRM approach to rural development (such as the GAAS team) have introduced innovations. We need to provide them with a favourable environment and guidance, which, of course, does not include top-down, purely theory-focused, boring lectures and useless courses, but dynamic, joint-learning experiences that allow exchange and sharing. Such a strategy is the way forward to mainstreaming collaborative learning and joint-action, not only in the university, but extended into the field. I was very happy to embark on this new journey, although worried about my limited experience, knowledge, and skills.

The initial planning workshop in Beijing on participatory curriculum development and mainstreaming of CBNRM (September 2004), with participants from China, Thailand, the Philippines, and Nepal, brought many like-minded people together. The workshop also allowed us to form a "mainstreaming" team at COHD, identify some concrete topics for a new CBNRM course, and distill important issues to be discussed further among the stakeholders. This was the first time that I experienced a curriculum development process initiated by a multidisciplinary team made up of university students and teachers, researchers from academies, and development practitioners from NGOs.

The fog covering the road was blown away slowly and I also became clearer about my role during this process. As a teacher with many years of experience in teaching graduates, I used to feel confused by the low levels of student satisfaction, despite having invested a lot of effort in curriculum development and delivery. Now I began to see that maybe facilitating the introduction of innovative teaching methods by a strong team of both teachers and students could lead to better results for the students.

Consultation with a number of graduates about their interests, views and needs concerning a CBNRM course and participatory curriculum development gave us strong support for our plan. We then organized the most exciting event of 2005 (in January) – the CBNRM course working group meeting. For all of us this was a new learning process of jointly preparing and delivering a completely novel course! The most impressive illustration of the impact of the workshop was the researcher, who, at the beginning of the three days questioned the possible contribution of student participants with so little field research experience; after two days of meeting, she smilingly answered her own question by affirming that it was possible. At that moment, I realized that we had embarked on a tough journey, but one with a possible bright destination. I also realized that we could make it happen if we would fully commit to what we stood for and remain responsible for what we would do. And, most important, we should believe in everyone's ability to be the agent of a strong miracle.

From a white sheet to a colourful drawing

Preparing the course materials helped me learn more about existing CBNRM research efforts, become familiar with potential partners and colleagues, and be more aware of the potential participation of the students. I also improved my understanding of development studies through lengthy discussions and debates with Xu Xiuli and Ronnie while preparing the course delivery in the classroom and villages and while guiding the students in their proposal development or in the assessment of their field experiences, reports, and CBNRM action proposals. No other courses that I have taught cost me so much energy and attention. Whenever I look back at the course development process, it always appears as a journey full of surprises, from a blank paper to a colourful picture, drawn collectively.

As the course coordinator, I discovered the importance of communication, rather than information delivery, among all participants. In addition, I realized the importance of the integration of existing ideas, concepts and theories, rather than simple knowledge accumulation or combination. It is still a long way to go to fully practice transformative learning, when the conventional roles of students and teachers remain so influential, but it is valuable and very feasible to try out this new way.

Along the way, critical reflection has accompanied us. We need to pay more attention to sharing our fruitful results and involve more and more students and researchers. We have to make more effort to report to the university, including the presidents, graduate school, undergraduate education department, the division of science and technology, and also make our work better known to other colleges. The Ministry of Education is carrying out a reform in higher education, with similar aims as our own. We have started paying more attention to its call for research projects, but we could do better. The first step in successful reform is that we received the support of our graduate school for our application on "Research on the innovation of RDM curriculum development and teaching methods." In this application, we highlighted another role of the CBNRM course in our RDM programme. We are thinking more and more about the implementation of a "responsible supervisor" system to provide supervision to graduates in a continuous and integrated manner, from the CBNRM course to the MSc. and Ph.D. thesis.

Fellowship support for the student's CBNRM fieldwork is an entry point to facilitate this link. The thesis supervisors of fellowship awardees began to understand more about the relevance of CBNRM research – an example of students showing teachers the way! As one of the supervisors, I am also benefiting from this management process. As part of the fellowship support, students are required to submit progress reports and encouraged to take part in exchange seminars. This series is more attractive than before, because of the chance to share experiences and lessons among almost all students in a very direct way, based on everybody's own thoughts and feelings.

Now, other universities, including JLAU, Hebei Agricultural University and Guangxi University, are following in our track. Through teacher-to-teacher and student-to-student dissemination, we are extending our approach and methods to other universities with a rural development programme (there are 28 of them in total).

I have learned a lot about the spiral-up process of awareness raising and behavioural change. This process is like a long road of change, in terms of discovering the theoretical contributions that action research can make, reconciling the conflict between short-term thesis research and longer-term action research, linking knowledge accumulation with practice, complementing different methodologies and teaching methods, acknowledging fully the roles of local communities and local people, and accepting everybody and believing in the potential contribution of everybody, including those who at the beginning do not show much active interest.

The value of more integrated capacity development approaches

"The five days in Ningxia reminded me of a proverb that says, 'A special place gives birth to special people.' The reality of rural life varies from place to place. When we saw the sand dunes and the soil walls of Kutuan village for the first time, some of us had an absurd thought: 'Why don't they all move into Yanchi County? Maybe it's a solution for their living.' But when we saw the enthusiastic peasants of Kutuan village, we changed our minds, because they had a common wish to develop their own village. The harmony among villagers impressed me deeply.

During the five days, we used participatory research tools to work with the peasants, and their warmness and real feelings touched me deeply. In the fieldwork that we did, I tried to play different roles, such as an interviewer, an anchor, a member of the PM & E group, and so on. Every role gave me different feelings. I think I will treasure these experiences, because it will help me a lot in the future. To us who are involved in the CBNRM course, we should consider the things that peasants pay attention to. In addition, we'd better guide peasants to use their own power and wisdom to overcome the development problems they face."

Zhang Ziqin, M.Sc. student, COHD, Beijing, March 2006

Natural resource management and rural development problems are complex, diverse, and in constant flux. Experiences from across China provide strong evidence of this (e.g., Yuan Juanwen and Sun

Qiu 2006, Song et al. 2006). Researchers are arguing that dynamic learning processes and methods are required to analyze these problems, carry out interventions, and assess alternatives (Vernooy et al. 2005). The challenge, then, is to do research that results in both a better understanding of the complexities of social life and a sounder base for action.

At the heart of such an approach is an effort to engage social actors and, together with those interested:

1. Set research priorities and identify key problems, issues, and opportunities.
2. Analyze the causes that underlie these problems and issues.
3. Take action to find both short- and long-term solutions to the identified problems or take advantage of opportunities.
4. Learn from these actions and make changes as needed.

Nowadays, management of major natural resources invariably creates situations in which various social actors operate, interact, and often debate and compete over the resources, interests, and points of view. Many researchers and practitioners in natural resource management are coming from the field of biophysics and do not have the social science skills and knowledge needed to work within a participatory research framework. The same can be said of many people involved in decision-making and policymaking.

Those working within a participatory research or development framework quickly realize that they must foster multi- and interdisciplinary ways of working. For many social scientists, this means gaining a better understanding of the natural sciences – histories, rationales, research questions, methods. It also requires working with partners from rural communities, as well as associated social actors or stakeholders, and speaking the same language about participatory action research in terms of approaches, tools, and practices.

Development and development research organizations, including those associated with the FCRN in China, have been trying to address the issues and challenges outlined above, usually with limited resources and support. Both researchers and practitioners (such as extensionists) have called for more and ongoing support. They are searching for clearer frameworks and sets of tools that enable them to improve their work with rural communities and other stakeholders in terms of effectiveness, scientific quality or rigour, and results.

Organizational obstacles and shortcomings – the lack of incentives, little or no recognition from peers – often hamper their work.

Elements of such frameworks as well as tools and techniques already exist, but they are scattered around organizations and countries. Many research and development organizations have experimented with various participatory research and training strategies, such as PM & E (Vernooy et al. 2003), social and gender analysis (Vernooy 2006), participatory development communication (Bessette 2004), use of the sustainable livelihoods framework, etc. However, most of these initiatives have focused on *individual* research capacity building (although some have also addressed team building). How this can be translated into more effective organizational capacity building remains a major question.

Knowledge about good practices for organizational research capacity building in CBNRM is still scarce. A few CBNRM-oriented organizations who are interested face challenges (Horton et al. 2003). Institutionalization is not something that results from a single research project or "policy brief," or even a series of publications, but only through a long-term consistent programme of support to partners for building capacity and gaining field experience. Our experiences are a good example.

Reflecting on this issue, staff at IDRC saw an opportunity to bring past and ongoing capacity development efforts and results together to institutionalize CBNRM in national or regional centres of excellence – places where future generations of CBNRM scholars, researchers, and practitioners could learn about, practice, improve, and disseminate CBNRM concepts, methods, and achievements. These ideas documented in a concept paper, presenting what was hoped was a series of clear and coherent ideas that could inspire the work done by us as well as that of partners (Bessette and Vernooy 2005). Later, when more confidence was gained on the usefulness of these ideas, an IDRC intern was asked to elaborate on the underlying thoughts more systematically and thoroughly (Large 2006).

"Centres" do not necessarily refer to physical units, such as university department. A centre could take the form of a network or a community of practice (Wenger 1998). The notion of moving *toward* centres of excellence emphasizes the institutional efforts required to ensure the promotion of CBNRM approaches, concepts, methods, and tools. As Wenger notes, this notion of "toward" implies action as the outcome of *cooperation* (mutual engagement) and *commitment to a common agenda*. Action is also informed by reflection, sometimes called praxis. It was hypothesized that these three elements – willingness to cooperate, shared goals, and continuous, collective reflection – are key to putting the concept of centres of excellence into practice.

In 2004, IDRC staff teamed up with Chinese colleagues to combine their ideas about mainstreaming CBNRM in higher education and the concept of centres of excellence, and put them into practice.

Magic at work (Part 1)

by Ronnie Vernooy, IDRC, Ottawa

When I think about our wonderful "CBNRM mainstreaming" experience, I travel back in time to my first visit to China in early 1999. Intrigued by the rapid changes occurring in the country and eager to learn more particularly, about how rural development was unfolding, I was very happy to accept an invitation from my now former IDRC colleague John Graham to accompany him to mountainous Yunnan and Guizhou provinces in the southwest. On that first visit, I met two of IDRC's CBNRM programme teams – from GAAS and Kunming Institute of Botany/Centre for Biodiversity and Indigenous Knowledge (KIB/CBIK) – and had a chance to see them in action (literally), working in the field together with poor and marginalized farmers, and struggling to give meaning to the notion of CBNRM as a new and more dynamic and holistic way to bring about change in rural China. This chance to visit a "new country," see it with my own eyes, and meet new colleagues touched my heart. I also became even more intrigued about the nature of the change processes underway, wondering about how the Chinese people would deal with the evident challenges, and what directions would enfold.

Growing roots

This first trip led to subsequent visits, and soon a new, joint GAAS-KIB/CBIK capacity development initiative was born. It would be the first project in China for which I carried full programme officer responsibility (for a detailed account of this initiative, see Vernooy et al. 2003). The project produced several "gifts": new colleagues and friends-in-the-making, i.e., some of the pioneers of CBNRM in China, and insights into the power of PM & E (see Vernooy et al. 2006). When John Graham retired a few years later, he kindly handed over to me the GAAS CBNRM project which served as one of the two case studies for the PM & E capacity development initiative. The GAAS project would become one of the cornerstones of the CBNRM course.

A subsequent visit brought me to the majestic, but congested, air-polluted, and (initially) overwhelming Beijing, where I was lucky to meet Li Xiaoyun (dean), Qi Gubo (who later occupied a central role in COHD), and other staff of the Center for Integrated Agricultural Development (CIAD), part of CAU. I could easily connect with the enthusiasm and dedication to participatory rural development of Xiaoyun and his team. In 2000, we joined forces to develop another new initiative, the Farmer-Centred Research Network (FCRN), which brought together staff of 12 agricultural/rural development organizations from across China, including colleagues from JLAU, GAAS, and HOPE in Ningxia. A small team from CIAD was delegated to take on networking coordination, technical support, and administration tasks. Gubo became FCRN coordinator in 2001 and, from then on, our interactions intensified. Our friendship grew at the same time.

After a short time interacting with CIAD staff, I remember having a very strong "aha moment" when I found out that several of them had strong intellectual, emotional, and professional connections to Wageningen Agricultural University in Holland, my own alma mater, in particular with Norman Long and his team of social-actor-oriented rural development social scientists. Being one of Norman Long's students, I had a strong feeling, in the presence of CIAD colleagues, of having returned "home." I think that the seed of connectivity and attachment to the CIAD team was planted at that moment. I would later often say that it was the power of the stars that brought us together … .

However, a solid spider web is not made with one or two threads. In 1999, through IDRC colleagues, I was put in touch with Yiching Song, a bright and audacious researcher from Guangxi province (in southwest China), who wanted to build on her Ph.D. research on the (missing) links between informal and formal seed systems, with a focus on maize. She expressed the wish to present a proposal to IDRC and the Ford Foundation, precisely, to do something about this disconnection, which was harming small farmers in Guangxi in particular. Although initially I was not supposed to be the programme officer for this new project, internal IDRC changes led me to assume programme officer responsibility during the development stage.

In 2000, the project was approved by the Ford Foundation and IDRC, providing me a link to the Center of Chinese Agricultural Policy (CCAP), the lead research organization (I would make a first visit to CCAP in 2002). CCAP had hired Yiching to bring more social science depth to its research agenda, moving beyond quantitative economics into rural development sociology. The link with Yiching and CCAP gave me another opportunity to gain first-hand knowledge about Chinese rural realities. At the same time, by working together on a visionary, challenging, but very rewarding initiative (what would become the first participatory plant breeding initiative in China; for details, see Vernooy 2003; Vernooy and Song 2004), we developed a very strong friendship – an unintended, but precious gift growing out of our professional work. The Guangxi project would become another of the cornerstones of the CBNRM course.

The capacity development strategy

The action research and capacity development efforts aim to make higher education more responsive to local communities and farmers needs. In concrete terms, it seeks to contribute to the capacity development of the current and next generations of rural development professionals and the other stakeholders involved in the effort. The design and delivery of new CBNRM curricula and related activities, which is expected to be expanded to the level of COHD's master's and Ph.D. programmes, are key means to bring about this innovation. Community-based, participatory field research, as part of the course, but also in the form of research for M.Sc. and Ph.D. theses, in turn, will provide the necessary inputs for the evolution of the curriculum.

The capacities that were identified to be developed or strengthened at both individual and organizational levels were:

1. The ability to work together with community members and other stakeholders, with a focus on the attitudes, knowledge, and skills to decide how to facilitate the planning, testing, and assessment of CBNRM research and development initiatives.
2. The knowledge, attitudes, and skills to apply participatory action research to practice (stakeholder analysis, consultation and planning, experimentation, monitoring and evaluation).
3. The ability to express clear views about participatory action research, link these views to field practices, and communicate

effectively about the development outcomes and impacts with others.

4. The ability to identify locally appropriate, effective individual and organizational capacity-building strategies.
5. The ability to apply a participatory curriculum development approach to reform the current teaching programmes and related research activities.
6. The knowledge and skills to manage participatory action research, teaching, training, and extension for CBNRM at the organizational level.

Informing these capacities is a way of learning as a collaborative learning-by-doing process through which *both* professional competence and personal identity can be enriched. It is envisioned that the introduction and experimentation with these new curricula and related field research practices will serve as a bridge to bring about changes on a large scale, at each of the universities in which the work is done, and beyond, at the level of national, higher-education policymaking. For these changes to occur, a more comprehensive mainstreaming strategy was developed step by step (Qi Gubo et al. 2008).

This capacity development plan has six interrelated components. At the core, is identification of "good practice" cases where participatory curriculum development is used for innovation in higher education and for introducing community-based, participatory rural development approaches. Participatory curriculum development is a method in which a number or all main social actors related to the subject are invited to take part in designing, planning, delivering, and assessing the curriculum. Similar to participatory action research approaches, this method aims to make the resulting learning more relevant and effective (Taylor 2003: 13). It follows a cyclical process involving five main steps – situational analysis/training needs assessments, framework design, detailed planning, delivery, assessment and possible refinement. At the heart of the method is teamwork, throughout the cycle and on.

The process includes continuing experimentation with the course at COHD in Beijing and a similar course at JLAU. It also includes support for similar course initiatives at other universities that are expected to emerge over time (By early 2007, four other universities in China, and three universities in Mongolia had joined these efforts). In addition, the use of participatory curriculum development in the creation of one or more other, related new courses at COHD and JLAU, possibly in cooperation with other departments within the university are envisioned. During the whole process, various stakeholders – students, teachers, farmers, local partners and officials – work together and learn from each other.

CBNRM course learning objectives

The courses at COHD and JLAU have a common learning structure, although they vary somewhat in terms of the actual delivery process, taking into consideration the different characteristics of the two universities. Both courses have specific but interrelated learning objectives achieved through connected modules. Each learning objective is defined in terms of leading to a "do-able" result, i.e., action-oriented. The 2008 CBNRM course objectives are listed in Box 10.

Box 10. Learning objectives for the 2008 CBNRM course at COHD

Module 1: Defining a CBNRM approach

At the end of Module 1, participants will be able to define the key elements of a CBNRM approach based on a review of selected international literature and guidance provided by the course facilitators, resulting in a coherent appreciation of interlinked concepts, principles, and methodology.

Module 2: Joint action learning in Chinese rural realities

At the end of Module 2, participants will be able to apply a CBNRM approach in actual rural situations in China, based on their own experiences, insights from Module 1, and self-selected field-research assignments.

Module 3: Reflecting on joint action learning in Chinese rural realities

At the end of Module 3, participants will be able to differentiate between effective and ineffective joint action-learning processes and methods, supported by selected literature, a comparative assessment of the field-research assignments carried out in Module 2, and the guidance of facilitators.

Module 4: Reviewing the international CBNRM literature

At the end of Module 4, participants will have identified elements from the international CBNRM literature applicable to research in the Chinese context, through critical individual reading combined with group discussion about self-selected references.

Module 5: Designing a CBNRM action-research proposal

At the end of Module 5, participants will be able to design a draft CBNRM action-research proposal, based on the results of modules 1, 2, and 3, and with the guidance of facilitators, adhering to the norms of clarity, coherence, relevance, and feasibility.

A second aspect of this activity is support for students and staff to allow them to link theory with community-based, participatory rural development practices, to reflect on and learn about these practices, and to use their field research results as inputs for course development and refinement. To make this happen, time and energy was invested in strengthening collaboration with the pioneers of CBNRM approaches in China, in particular with colleagues at partner organizations, such as the Guizhou Academy of Agricultural Sciences, the Center for Chinese Agricultural Policy, the NGO HOPE in Ningxia, and others. Linking with the colleagues who are also part of the FCRN has been crucial. Long-term, field-based action research, networking, and mainstreaming in higher education are coming together in their initiative. Over time, and through learning by doing, a stronger "community" of learning was seen to be evolving.

This support component is implemented through small-grant fellowship support for students carrying out research for their thesis, supervision of students by COHD and JLAU staff jointly with the partner organizations mentioned above, a seminar series with students and interested staff (run by students) including people outside COHD and JLAU, and a publication series. The fellowship provides support to master's students for four months of study in the field and to Ph.D. students for six months. Students who receive fellowship support usually live in a village, eat what farmers eat, and often help with the farm work, from planting to harvesting rice. They learn not only how to work with farmers and local partners and to collect necessary information for research, but also to make a meaningful contribution to the village and farmers in terms of rural development.

The third component is supporting CBNRM and PRD fieldwork to link theory with practice, to allow students and staff to reflect on and learn from these activities, and to enable them to use the results of field research as inputs for course development and refinement. This means strengthening collaboration with CBNRM pioneers, such as Guizhou Academy of Agricultural Sciences, the Centre for Chinese Agricultural Policy, Centre for Biodiversity and Indigenous Knowledge, and others. This component is implemented through small-grant support for thesis fieldwork, supervision of CBNRM and PRD students by COHD and JLAU staff jointly with partners, a seminar series with students and interested staff, including those outside COHD and JLAU, and a publication series.

Turning to the external context, the fourth element concerns the creation of an enabling environment. This means accessing and guaranteeing long-term financial and political support from Chinese sources, such as CAU and JLAU administrators, the Ministry of Education, the Ministry of Agriculture, perhaps with complementary funding from donor agencies. This component will be operationalized through policy research, analysis, and advocacy efforts. The intent is to make our research more responsive to the needs of policymakers, especially those involved in the higher education reform policy currently being implemented (Box 11).

Box 11. Higher education policy reform underway

The Ministry of Education is currently implementing an ambitious and wide-ranging policy reform process to respond to changing societal demands. The new policy directions are based on the observation that China's society is changing rapidly and the traditional way of organizing and managing the higher education system is no longer adequate to deal with these changes. There is a clear recognition that an education system based on a rigid, top-down planned approach will no longer provide the country with the necessary human resources "to achieve modernization" (Zhou Ji 2006: xiii).

The new policy covers the establishment of academic specialties, reform of the mode of student training, strengthening of teaching management, strengthening of character education in universities, reform in how English is taught, and adjustment of curricula.

Overall, the new policy provides a supportive macro-framework for our mainstreaming initiative, but a number of challenges and difficulties are also evident. Later in this chapter, we identify some of them and suggest ways to deal with these "roadblocks."

The fifth component of this work is the sharing of experiences, results, and lessons. This is being accomplished through regular exchange events, within the universities, among universities, and among universities and other stakeholders. An experimentation with a teacher-to-teacher and student-to-student approach, similar to the farmer-to-farmer approach used by extension workers is done. Reflecting on these experiences and using these reflections to improve the work is one of the good-practice principles that is being promoted.

Lastly, building on the key role of reflection is the use of sound, ongoing, PM & E (Vernooy et al. 2003). In this case, it is a joint effort by staff, students, and others, such as farmers, government officials, and extension workers, to monitor and evaluate, systematically, all the activities. This implies, firstly, strengthening the PM & E skills through targeted training and practice and the development and implementation of sound monitoring and evaluation plans. Experimenting with such a monitoring and evaluation approach is at the heart of this efforts.

A journey filled with emotion (Part 1)

by Zhang Li, COHD, Beijing

My story begins in January 2005, when the first CBNRM planning workshop was held in China. I heard about it from Li Xiaoyun, the dean of our college [COHD], and he suggested me to attend the workshop, though I did not know anything about it.

It was an amazing yet painful time. I never had any idea that students could also be involved in curriculum development. I was amazed by what we did during the workshop together with the teachers. But, it was also a tough experience for me. The context, the way of thinking, and the relationship between teachers and students were new. The workshop enlightened me so much that I felt I have grown wiser. I accepted the idea of a "learner-centred" approach, which I thought was the dream of many students. I was hopeful that every course development initiative would use a "participatory" method.

However, I did not take the 2005 [CBNRM] course, because I was in the second year of my M.Sc., and my specialization was in regional economics. My thesis was about "enterprise development," which is in no way related to CBNRM. And, at the planned time of the CBNRM course, I intended to do my fieldwork.

In June 2005, I was fortunate to get a chance to "jump" to Ph.D. studies in Rural Development and Management, starting in September 2005. When I had to choose courses for the first year of my Ph.D., I selected the CBNRM course as the first one, and my fruitful CBNRM journey started.

I entered the 2006 CBNRM planning workshop on my own initiative. Because I had participated in the 2005 workshop, I could easily follow what was going on. Afterwards, I confirmed my selection of the course and, at the same time, I became one of the three course assistants. There were two reasons for choosing the course. One was curiosity to know more about the course context and the delivery method. The other was the new atmosphere, characterized by the facilitators' attitudes, their readiness to open their hearts, and their friendliness.

The course turned out to be difficult for me than I had thought. It required me to put my heart into it. As an assistant, I was busier than the other students. I had to take care not only of the learning context, but also of some logistic work. I learned to manage time, and thought about how to work efficiently and effectively. This way I gained a lot in terms of CBNRM professional skills.

In addition, I also formed my own technique about how to do the organizational work. I feel proud of that. This course gave me a lot of space to carry out my own ideas.

More practice, more experience

After the course, I asked myself why I put more effort into the CBNRM course than any other course. I think the most important reason is that it made me change from passively accepting learning to actively participating, by changing the relationship between teachers and students, creating horizontal communication, and encouraging students to express their own thinking.

The course is not only delivered in the classroom, but also offers a chance to do a field study, to put the theory into practice. The field study took me into the vivid world of farmers' lives. Talking with farmers, living with them, learning from them, and sharing with them – there are much more interesting things in the real world than in a textbook.

Until I was in the field, I did not understand the meaning of "learning by doing". Once I did an interview with two farmers, who sat in their chairs, and I stood in front of them while talking. Luckily, my supervisor came to me and suggested that I sit down. When I sat down the interview became easier for all of us. You can learn the concepts and methods from a textbook, but learning through practice is always helpful.

Another gift from the field study was the identification of the research question for my Ph.D. dissertation. Before the course, I used to find a research question through a literature review. But the course taught me to pick up question based one real life. In this way, the research questions are more related to the farmers' livelihoods and, thus, the research that follows can be more effective for farmers.

Linked to the course were many other activities, such as exchange visits with JLAU students, the fellowship support programme, and the writing workshop in December 2006 to guide us in our thesis writing. All these activities opened my eyes, making me braver and more confident. An interesting story would help to explain this.

In January 2007, I had a chance to take part in the first writing workshop to prepare this book, in Singapore. During the workshop, I made a presentation to local IDRC staff introducing our efforts in capacity development. During the first 10 minutes, many things happened to me. The first problem I was worried about was language. All the people there spoke excellent English, but I have no confidence in my English. I hid my nervousness, and began with a smile. I let myself face the audience and tried to contact everybody with my eyes. Then I saw someone fall asleep, and another one seemed impatient. "Is my presentation boring?" Suddenly, I felt depressed and wanted to finish quicker. I turned my head to the screen, and did not look at the people. But, when I turned back, a smiling face full of encouragement rushed into my eyes, as if saying, "Come on, someone is listening carefully, put your heart into it and continue!" I smiled again and finished my presentation. In the end, I outdid myself and became more confident. This experience will accompany me my whole life.

In addition, I want to highlight two things – teamwork and friendship. Without the friendship and teamwork created throughout this experience, nothing could have happened. Through friendship, I learned how to cooperate with other partners and how to find my position. The progress of the whole team is creating a better environment for every member and this, in turn, is providing more chance to develop oneself.

Other things are still to come. I will be one of the co-facilitators for the 2007 CBNRM course, and I am sure that it will be another exciting journey.

Part 2: Changes in capacity – the results so far

> "My fieldwork is going well. I have gathered a lot of information that is very important for my thesis. I interviewed different people in the field, such as farmers, village cadres, and local officials. I lived in a farmer's house. I have learned a lot, for example, how to communicate with people with whom you are not familiar, how to obtain true information, how to live in a harsh environment, and so on. I also faced some difficulties in the field. At first I was not welcomed by the people there, especially the local officers. They were not willing to provide materials and it was hard to get data from them. Secondly, there was a feeling of lonliness and helplessness in the field. The investigator suffers a psychological torment. I think it is normal when one is living in a new environment as an outsider. But the experience can make one stronger."
>
> *M.Sc. student, Beijing, September 2006*

By summer 2007, 125 postgraduate students in Beijing and Changchun had taken part in the new CBNRM and PRD courses and related field research, accompanied by a total of 20 facilitator-teachers who were directly involved in the process. For the two courses in 2008, another 50 students have applied. At the field level, numerous farmers, extensionists, government staff, leaders, researchers, and research managers have also been involved in these efforts. Colleagues at CAU, JLAU, and collaborating organizations in China (notably the Centre for Chinese Agricultural Policy, Guizhou Academy of Agricultural Sciences, HOPE, the Guangxi Maize Research Institute, Yunnan University's Regional Development Research Centre) and elsewhere (CIP-UPWARD and IDRC) have provided strong direct and indirect support – technical, administrative, logistic, and financial. Our involvement in this process has been extraordinary, leading to many new insights and experiences.

In this second part of the case study, the main changes that have occurred at the individual and organizational levels are described, with a focus on what might be called the interpersonal or micro-organizational level. A distinction between strengthened capacities in terms of changes in attitudes, knowledge, and skills, and the resulting practice or performance, are made individually and organizationally. A number of unexpected outcomes are also being identified. The learning encompasses many new conceptual (including attitudinal), methodological, and practical (behavioural) elements. It has also started to lead to what can be thought as various expressions of transformative learning, i.e., more encompassing ways of adapting to new circumstances, designing one's own path of life, and learning about learning itself. The initial achievements and insights are finding their way to other places as well, both inside and outside China. The summary of the learning achievements includes changes occurring at the local level as well, as perceived by ourselves and by our partners in various parts of the country.

Developing professional skills

> "I feel with the help of this course I learned a lot about the content, principles, and methods of CBNRM. My knowledge and perception of related theories have deepened by virtue of the field visit that the course demanded. A thorough study of CBNRM has also given me new insight into the research mechanism in the field of participation, such as identifying problems, establishing concepts of participation and empowerment, considering participation from a gender perspective, building participation capacity in various strata of participants, integrating participation projects into the communities, and building trust and teamwork into implementation of participatory development. Through theoretical and practical study, I also have an explicit understanding of action research. Compared with conventional courses, we are more involved and affected by CBNRM studies."
>
> *Ph.D. student, COHD, Beijing, April 2006*

A golden rule applied throughout the course development process, was "no lectures, no lecturing." We stuck to this principle to encourage learning through active discovery. This allowed us to combine theoretical insights that support CBNRM – for example, from rural development sociology, agro-ecology, and political science – with practice. As one of the students summarized, "I learned a new way of learning by doing. This is a very good method for field study." Doing includes "simple" things like communicating with others, in the classroom and in the field.

"In the course, I began to show more enthusiasm and take more initiative. I understand that what I have said is listened to carefully by others and recorded. Both the students and teachers seemed to be interested in what I said and made comments and suggestions." Many of the students mentioned that the course gave them a chance to make friends – with peers and with farmers, government officers, and extensionists. As one stated, "Friendship is the most unexpected fortune that I will cherish."

The course and fieldwork began the process of developing the skills needed for valuing and, more importantly, *using* a CBNRM approach in today's rural China. These skills include the ability to analyze situations and problems from a people's perspective using a holistic and interdisciplinary scientific approach, combining natural and social science knowledge and methods, and keeping a critical eye on the socioeconomic and sociopolitical dimensions of natural resource management and rural development at large. Students and staff improved their ability to define CBNRM-oriented research questions and develop action-focused research proposals. From a struggle to define research questions in the first place, students have come a long way.

But the stimulating exercises in the class and the strong emotions generated by the fieldwork also opened eyes to the "darker" side of working for rural development. Many students increased their (theoretical) understanding of participatory action research and CBNRM, but observed that practicing it adequately is still a major challenge. This is not surprising, given the short duration of the course and field assignment. The focus on the social dimensions of CBNRM (e.g., Module 3 on effective and ineffective action-learning processes) contributed to "seeing the process, troubles, conflicts and influences of participatory rural development."

The importance and the power of full engagement was (re) discovered, not only during course delivery, but also in the management of the whole process. This is strikingly summarized by Yang Huan, one of the 2006 CBNRM course assistants:

> It is not easy for me to talk about my feelings in this course. The most important thing that I want to say is what someone else said: "You can learn more from the process if you take part in the course more actively." I took part in the January 2006 workshop for curriculum development ... . As a student, this course is really novel for us. It is

interesting and open. The thing that impresses me most is the power of the team. If you change one apple with someone else's apple, each of you still has only one apple; if you change an idea with another, both of you have two ideas. The formulation of the survey plan in the field, the report, the proposal, the short movie [of the field visit], all give me many new things. It is really learning by doing. And the course persists in emphasizing the practice. (Beijing, April 2006)

The insistence on learning by doing contributed to the formation of stronger character – the emergence of several new student "champions". Giving these champions the chance to practice what they learned and learn more was very important in deepening the experience. This requires creating opportunities and providing mentoring support.

The persistent link between theory and practice contributed to a greater ability to define the key concepts, principles, and methods of CBNRM, one of the main learning objectives of the course (specifically of Module 1, but reiterated throughout all modules). Students phrased this as "CBNRM becoming more meaningful."

"I have completed the 2006 CBNRM course from which I learned a lot, such as learning-by-doing and teamwork. I learned many participatory research methods and mastered farmer-centred research methods in the field survey. And I know how to share research results and learning experience with team members and how to promote cooperation through teamwork. I would like to continue along this path."

Ph.D. student, COHD, Beijing, April 2006

Emancipatory learning

"When I returned from Baicheng, I was depressed again by the life model that I have now. I miss life in Baicheng and I miss our course. The course aroused great feelings in me. I could participate freely and actively especially when I worked with the farmers and the government staff. I think these experiences and feelings will effect my life. When I become a University teacher, by applying these methods I would make my students enjoy my class."

M.Sc. student, JLAU, Changchun, May 2006

Apart from improving technical knowhow (research techniques) and practical knowledge (research management), the project is contributing to emancipatory knowledge. By this we mean the capacity to become more aware and critical of ourselves and our environment and to transform reality through action. Mezirow and associates (2000; see also Cranton 2006) describe the various interrelated dimensions of personal development and transformation as follows – the capacity to engage with the world of ideas and learn from experience, to challenge one's own assumptions; to arrive at thoughtful commitment through self-reflection; to construct a value system that informs behaviour and to risk action based on these values; to contribute one's voice to a collective endeavour, realizing that collective awareness and thinking are greater than the sum of their parts; and to become a continuous learner, e.g., by seeking authentic feedback from others.

In this case, the most visible expressions of this kind of change were students who changed from passive listeners to active contributors, from sitting "second row" to sitting around the table with facilitator-teachers – and with government officials in the field. They evolved from simply looking up to facilitator-teachers to sharing thoughts with them, sometimes even fiercely contradicting them. Many of them learned not to be nervous in front of a large group of students or farmers, even when deans, directors, or other high-ranking officials were present, and to speak their minds and share their thoughts and experiences. Eating together with staff (instead of eating separately), while seemingly trivial, was of considerable symbolic importance and was also part of the change. Students themselves facilitated activities, such as small group discussions, and organized and led many of the monitoring and evaluation sessions.

Being involved in the whole development process (the course and fellowship support), which was characterized by cycles of action and reflection, also allowed many to become more aware of their own different backgrounds, knowledge, and skills. Through the various iterations, they strengthened their reflective skills. This is helping them become more adept at adjusting and adapting along the way and, more effective and less prone to mistakes.

The relevance of CBNRM to the many problems embedded in the complex and rapidly changing rural realities across China – and the potential solutions was discovered. As a result, the sense of the dynamic roles are sharpened that rural development professionals can play in today's rapidly changing China. Involvement in the courses and related field research guides to a new perspective on the studies and work, central to which are the connections with each other and with the people with whom cooperation in rural areas across the country takes place. These connections have led to the mobilization of energy toward change – in the classroom and in the field.

More cognizance of the small but important contributions that each can make to collective efforts is seen. This is highlighted, first, by a radical shift from a teacher-centred to a learner-centred approach to learning. This has been into practice in the everyday course dynamics, the physical set-up of the classroom, exercises in the class and in the field, and in the nature of facilitator – student interactions as well as those between facilitators and students and the people with whom they interact, such as villagers in the rural areas where they do their research.

There is also greater emphasis on the potential power of teamwork and friendship, which can create strong synergies. Throughout the courses, the fellowship support programme, and the related activities, learners were able to discover the notion that the whole can be more than the sum of the parts. In addition, through enthusiastic involvement, new friendship was also made, not only among peers, but also between facilitator-teachers and students. The relevance of teamwork, or more broadly, collective action, in the field as well, as a key element in resolving natural resource management problems, tensions, and conflicts was understood. Many are now trying to apply this insight in a practical way, as part of research, policy reform, and development initiatives in various parts of the country in collaboration with local partners.

Managing the change process

> "The most important thing is to have a mechanism to improve the course according to the suggestions and advice from different stakeholders. The form might not be the most important. The most important thing is to make every teacher really respect the suggestions and advice from different stakeholders and make other stakeholders willing to participate. In the current system, course evaluation is just a form; no one really cares about students' needs. And evaluation forms are too rigid. But the CBNRM course gives us an example of how to solve this problem. Everyone feels that they are the master of the course. Teachers are not afraid to look at the different needs of different students. So everyone feels very happy in the CBNRM course."
>
> *Yang Huan, 2006 CBNRM course assistant, January 2007*

It is seen that bringing about change requires mutual engagement and commitment or passion for a common undertaking that has clear goals that have been agreed on jointly – a common *course*. At the same time, it was discovered that conducting such a change process, requires creating and constantly nurturing an enabling environment – in the classroom, in the field, and beyond, among both students and facilitator-teachers, during informal conversations, meetings, workshops, and with others with whom interaction happens during work, such as farmers and government staff. Central to this enabling environment is the space to freely express oneself – feelings as well as thoughts – to be heard with attention and respect, and to be given the opportunity to ask questions.

A very important feature has been the chance to interact equally, irrespective of social status defined by position, age, and sex, and to participate and contribute to the best of one's ability irrespective of level of expertise. In the context of the still strong Chinese cultural values and norms of authority, power, and respect for teachers, this has perhaps been one of the biggest changes that was brought about.

The learner-centred arrangement of the classroom, the "ice-breaking" puzzle game at the beginning of the CBNRM and PRD courses, role playing, regular teamwork (replacing individual learning), the reflective audiovisual presentations produced by students, and peer review of project proposals have all proved to be key methods contributing to the ambiance. The meaningful inclusion of students in the establishment and administration of the courses – as members of the working group, assistants, and apprentice facilitators – as core members of the fellowship support management team, and as part of the monitoring and evaluation and documentation processes is another crucial element. Not only did students contribute time and energy to the pioneering efforts, they also effectively allowed sharing of expertise between the "older" participants and the younger ones, between the current and the coming generation of rural development professionals.

Linking theory to practice

According to most students, the course contributed, to varying degrees, to their ability to link the CBNRM–PRD approach to actual rural situations in China, to design and draft a CBNRM action-research proposal, and, especially for the Ph.D. students at COHD, to review international literature in relation to the CBNRM course.

"I am majoring in rural development management. I have been to some poor rural areas in several provinces as a consultant or researcher and have found a lot of poor people improved their livelihood with external support especially with the help of development projects, which affirm participatory approaches. I think action research is one of the most effective ways to put theory/ideas into practice and make things change. So I hope I can apply what I learned from the CBNRM course and make a contribution to rural development. I don't want to be a researcher who only speaks and does not convert it to action."

Ph.D. student, COHD, Beijing, April 2006

"The trip to Guangxi was unforgettable. Friendship with local farmers and also with our 'family,' the party with farmers, the local team, and our family are all kept in my mind. All these encourage me to continue."

Ph.D. student, COHD, Beijing, March 2006

The various field visits and follow-up research carried out by a number of the students generated not only research results, but also deep feelings and strong memories. The open, largely self-directed, and intense engagement with the complexities of rural life in Ningxia, Guizhou, Guangxi, and Jilin has marked most if not all of the students (and facilitator-teachers as well). For many – as the vivid and often heartwarming testimonials tell – the visits were beyond their expectations. For some, it was the first prolonged stay in a rural area, not based on rapidly "extracting information" for the sake of fulfilling a task assigned by someone else. For almost all students, it was the first joint research exercise, based on interactions with local partners and driven by a desire to learn something, share thoughts, ideas, and experiences, and explore possible future cooperation in terms of mutual interests, but respectful of local agendas and circumstances.

For the courses and field research, the use of a variety of teaching and research tools was encouraged. During the courses, methods included case study analysis and comparison of cases, critical literature review, group proposal writing, group reporting of field research, audiovisual presentation of fieldwork, puzzle games, and role playing.

During the field research, students, with some guidance from facilitator-teachers, used a variety of tools usually including individual and group interviews, participatory mapping (of the natural resource base or social networks and organizational context), participatory ranking exercises, participant observation, group discussion, photographing and videotaping, and role playing (as a feedback tool). PM & E tools were used throughout the process. Facilitators stressed that practice – experimenting with a variety of tools – is very important.

Students understood and appreciated the need to learn a number of methods and practice using them, as evidenced by some of their comments CBNRM course evaluation reports of 2005–2008:

> Through practice, I mastered methods, which I have never used before.
>
> I learned some new skills and used some new tools during the field visit, and I have more willingness to develop or study now.
>
> How to do a field visit, how to communicate with local people: I have learned a lot in the village. I also know PM & E is a good method.
>
> I learned more about self-reflection and others' merits through the fieldwork.
>
> The active learning and teaching style are beyond my expectations, such as the puzzle game and the role-play.

The power of teamwork

Joint or collective efforts are at the heart of the course, not only because this mirrors one of the pillars of CBNRM – the notion of "community-based" management – but also because it is considered central to the process of learning itself. According to Wenger (1998), teamwork is central as a means to explore and experiment with forms of mutual engagement (how to work together effectively and efficiently); define, negotiate, and stick to a common agenda (how to carry out an exercise according to agreed on rules); and develop a "track record" of progress and achievements (producing accounts, representations, stories). Teamwork has several dimensions and is very fruitful, as students and facilitator-teachers have mentioned CBNRM course evaluation reports of 2005–2008:

> The friendly atmosphere makes me happy to work with the facilitators, my classmates, and local officials and farmers. It is a process of learning, including gaining knowledge and developing friendship.
>
> I got a lot of inspiration from other team members.
>
> The teamwork was beyond my expectations. I can see the power of teamwork and how it can become an important idea.
>
> Through teamwork I learned a lot from others. I have made some good friends.
>
> From the course I learnt that students and teachers can become very good friends. This will make me communicate with them and express my suggestions more actively.
>
> The course has brought me a new attitude, which can support and direct my future research. Teamwork is the biggest gift for me. We have become good friends.

More than just friendship, the word "family" frequently appears in the testimonials of participants. Bonding takes place in the classroom through the collective work, among the 25–30 students and 5–10 facilitator-teachers and, especially, in the field within the groups of 8–10 students and 2–3 facilitator-teachers. Traveling together was a first time experience for many students and working intensively together in a remote area, trying to carry out a research task brought participants together. Careful guidance and the systematic use of process monitoring have played an important role in this process. When tensions, problems, or conflicts arise, the groups try to deal with them immediately by sitting together to reflect on what happened and why. No one is blamed, but suggestions for alternative behaviour are solicited, reviewed, and when "approved" put into practice. From learning to work together to defining and carrying out tasks in an effective way, students and facilitators, alike, shift to learning together based on friendship and "family" ties (for a more detailed discussion, see Cranton 2006: 42–43).

Reflecting on teamwork in terms of a broader innovation perspective (Wenger et al. 2002), it was suggested that the horizontally oriented, self-organizing nature of the working and learning groups had much to do with the positive achievements. Assigning tasks and responsibility as much as possible to the practitioners themselves is another key feature. Collegial relations are the focus, but not reporting relations. This approach produces knowledge that is "close to the ground," with an immediate use. Too often still, academic knowledge is disconnected from real life and students are seen as cheap labour for teachers.

Teamwork takes time and effort and does not always proceed without problems. Working groups discovered that not all team members speak up and contribute. PM & E groups suggested giving "shy" students more opportunities to do a presentation. Efforts were usually made to address this problem, but it merits systematic attention from all participants. Some students observed that during the course, teamwork had been very good, but cooperative behaviour did not necessarily continue outside the classroom. They thought that the learning process should emphasize the fact that cooperation does not end at the classroom.

Magic at work (Part 2)

by Ronnie Vernooy

Action learning

Gubo has described how the two ideas for a mainstreaming initiative (from COHD and IDRC) came together. Although based on a radical vision and a long-term action and higher education reform agenda, the initial proposal we put together was modest in scope. We hypothesized that only through joint action (based on a new way of working together and on forming a new network of like-minded and like-hearted people) would we be able to assess more clearly whether a participatory curriculum development process would work in today's China. Only later, after we had learned a lot from our first CBNRM course experience in 2005 and when, by luck, IDRC provided additional resources, we designed a more ambitious agenda. And so I was enrolled, step by step, in an incredibly rich learning experience. All along, it has been through action, and trial and error, that we learned what we could bring about. Looking back now, this is an important insight.

I had much to learn ... which I knew from the very first day. I had some facilitation experience, but very little formal teaching knowhow. As a university student, I took part in a participatory M.Sc. level course-redesign effort, which, although more than 20 years had passed, still provided inspiration and guidance. I did not speak or read Chinese, and could only understand a little. I still knew little about rural China. I had CBNRM-oriented field-research experience, both first- and second-hand, through my own fieldwork and through involvement in many IDRC-supported initiatives. But CBNRM is still a new field. What I could contribute most was enthusiasm and a certain convening power, i.e., bringing people together to join forces and open up new roads. Jingsong Li summarized these capacities as – "More encouragement, more work." I cannot argue with this apt description.

Along the way, the many encounters have played a crucial role in our collective and individual learning processes. In these encounters, facilitated by members of the working groups taking turns, we encouraged everyone to open their minds and hearts to each other, search for a common purpose, envision and actualize new ties, and work toward "unthinkable realities." We encouraged everyone, including and especially the courageous students who joined us (Zhang Li was among the very first), to move into action and get started, without having doctored out the details of our plans. After every small step, both confidence and commitment grew. Discovering the power of this "movement" and building on it was one of the important things I learned over time.

18–19 January, 2005, will always remain memorable because the initiative we had planted began to take root on this date. About twenty of us, including Gubo and Zhang Li, came together to design a new CBNRM course. This is what I wrote later:

"The planning workshop was a challenge, in particular, because this was the first time that COHD staff and students would be interacting and working on equal terms toward a common goal, from the very beginning of an initiative. I think that the workshop went very well, both in terms of results and process, i.e., participation, working together on equal terms."

"I am very pleased with the draft course design. It is innovative, coherent, and feasible, and represents a unique approach to postgraduate learning. I wish that I had taken courses like this when I was a postgraduate student!"

"The ambiance during the workshop was very good and stimulating, and we made good progress in building friendships (another objective defined). Our efforts to respect everyone and to provide space for more or less equal and fair participation had a lot to do with this. This is perhaps one of the major outcomes: the building of an action group committed to introduce a new way of learning at COHD."

"We could have tried harder to share time and responsibilities among the group of facilitators/teachers. Unfortunately, we did not meet before the workshop to discuss dynamics and tasks. This is something to improve next time."

"All in all, I thought it was an extraordinary workshop, which I enjoyed very much, and which took place in a very up-beat atmosphere. Results were outstanding and included a sound basis for further preparations and the actual delivery of the course."

Learning from the new generation

Each subsequent year we organized a planning workshop, to bring together the new course working group, get to know each other better, and plan the year's course in detail. Learning from the previous year, we always adjust workshop dynamics accordingly. So far, in each new cycle a number of extraordinary MSc. and PhD. students have joined the group, quickly becoming part of the CBNRM family. Interacting with them, working with them, studying and researching with them has been a very enriching experience for me. Having this opportunity to accompany, in a small way, the coming generation of rural development professionals in their postgraduate studies, has given a new direction to my work as an IDRC programme officer. I see the sharing ideas and experiences with them as giving concrete meaning to that noble concept of sustainability.

In the course, inspired and guided by a committed core group of staff and students (with new faces each year), we do some pretty "crazy" things, at least according to conventional Chinese teaching methods. We play games, use role play, work with photos and videos, integrate PM & E from the beginning, go into the field together to carry out a collectively designed research task, sing and dance, cry sometimes, and study and research together intensely. "So much teamwork," one of the student's once remarked.

Each year I do my best to help facilitate one or more of the five modules. In 2005 and 2006, I worked with Gubo and other teachers, but last year (2007), mostly with our "champion" students of that moment, including Zhang Li. The others were Zhang Ziqin, Liu Yuhua, and Yang Huan. I am learning "to give all of myself" in the course, in the classroom in particular. In the field, although always mindfully present as well, I keep a low profile and let the students manage the learning process by themselves, "intervening" only sporadically, for example, when they really get badly "stuck" (even then, the farmers usually have very subtle ways of guiding the students through such moments). Together with the small contributions I have also made to the JLAU courses, I begin to feel more confident about my new career as a "teacher." To paraphrase a Chinese saying, the more you give, the more you get.

Encouraged and often revitalized by their experiences, many of the students who participate in the CBNRM course, decide to focus their M.Sc. or Ph.D. thesis fieldwork on CBNRM issues and questions as well. A growing number are benefiting from the fellowship support programme, which I helped design, based on previous IDRC experiences. Each year, I have had the chance to co-supervise several students, which is another source of continuous learning. Interacting with them during the whole research process, from proposal writing to defence (and in some cases, beyond, i.e., in the search for a job), is giving me deeper insights in the dynamics of being a student and researcher in China, while at the same time giving me a broader view on the rural development processes as they play out in various parts of the country. With each of the students whom I co-supervise, it is as if I am doing my own M.Sc. and Ph.D. again. The marvellous thing is that, experiences, insights, new ideas, and friendships are broadening continuously while at the same time making the web denser.

I have completed ten years in China in January (2009). I could not have imagined that I would become so deeply involved and be befriended by so many of the country's inspiring (young) people in a collective journey toward making rural development more sustainable and rural development studies and research more relevant and interesting. In this journey, more dynamic, horizontal, and meaningful patterns of working together continue to evolve; new ideas keep popping up, and our vision and efforts to innovate is now spreading to other universities in the country, and in to the neighbouring Mongolia as well. In each place, sparks are flying, inspired by our experience, guiding principles, and methods, but giving a particular local shape to the CBNRM mainstreaming initiative. May this magic journey continue.

Toward organizational change

Collective efforts are at the heart of the CBNRM course. According to Wenger (1998), teamwork is central to exploring and experimenting with forms of mutual engagement; defining, negotiating, and keeping to a common agenda; and developing a "track-record" of progress and achievements (producing accounts, representations, stories). The process of becoming a team – developing companionship and friendship as much as sharing work – does merit more attention than usually acknowledged in participatory curriculum development theory. Teams do not just form and continue to exist; their members must continue to make connections and establish a "track-record," in Wenger's sense.

Working groups have been crucial in managing the whole process of CBNRM mainstreaming. However, team formation required to know each other and establish connections – among colleagues from quite different organizations, among the "daring" students, and, most likely of all, among staff and students, who traditionally, seldom interact in non-hierarchical and non-instrumental ways.

All our efforts combined are gradually bringing about changes at the organizational level, within CAU and at JLAU (more slowly and with a more limited scope so far), but also in some of the partner organizations, most notably the Center for Chinese Agricultural Policy, the Guizhou Academy of Agricultural Sciences, and the NGO HOPE. These changes concern key elements of organizational development – communications; management; leadership; programming; incentives and rewards; and networking. At CAU and JLAU, as well as at other collaborating universities such as Hebei, Guangxi, Guiyang, and Kunming, we see students becoming more vocal and assuming a stronger role in their courses and other study activities. In December 2006, in Beijing, for example, a group of M.Sc. and Ph.D. students initiated a comprehensive assessment of all their courses, in terms of content and dynamics, with the aim of bringing about changes and improvements.

Staff taking part in the CBNRM courses at CAU and JLAU have started to make changes in other courses they are teaching, including at the undergraduate level. They are also developing innovative ideas to apply to some of their existing courses and perhaps to develop new courses later. Other members of the course working groups have carried their experiences home – to Guizhou, Guangxi, Yunnan, and Mongolia, and have begun to integrate key elements and experiences from the CBNRM courses into their own teaching and training efforts. Current work and the success achieved at CAU and JLAU are attracting the interest of other universities in China and abroad – in Vietnam and Laos as well as Mongolia. Through IDRC involvement, wider links are also being developed – in Asia and even Africa.

Contributions to rural development

It has proved very effective to adapt course content and dynamics to the local level – analyzing situations from local people's perspectives, asking relevant questions, combining natural and social science elements, and dealing with socioeconomic and political dimensions of natural resource management, such as differences in knowledge, resources, and conflicts. Linking the courses and field research directly to local-level rural development issues and initiatives is a key path by which bringing higher education closer to reality and making a difference is envisioned. Based on observations and analysis so far, it is believed that the efforts are contributing to modest change in a number of ways.

Students contribute to more relevant research and to some action at the local level. The most dominant research theme chosen by CBNRM–PRD students has been the key issue of farmer organization, encompassing economic, sociocultural, and political elements. They have worked directly with village development committees, cooperatives, local agricultural research committees, associations, and cultural performance groups in a number of provinces. Their research and related efforts have focused on strengthening these organizations to give farmers more opportunities and influence (Box 16).

> **Box 12. Helping farmers organize and improve their livelihoods**
>
> Two of COHD's M.Sc. students provide an example of small-scale action, though not entirely related to their research. In Guangxi, villagers were experiencing decreasing cassava yields. The students facilitated a meeting of the farmers and local research partners to discuss the problem and generate some suggestions for action. The villagers were interested in diversifying and trying, for example, Chinese herbs as an alternative crop. Some of the villagers joined forces to prepare a small experiment and investigate marketing options. The students offered ideas and some small financial support. The experiment is now underway in the village. Many farmers, who originally did not take part in the discussions, have now joined the group that set up the experiment. At first curious about the novelty, they quickly realized it could benefit everyone.

The students stay, live, and work with farmers during their fieldwork for both the course and thesis research. For the latter, this offers them a unique opportunity to learn in more depth about rural life and the changes occurring in rural areas all over the country. They all try, in one way or another, to become part of the community and learn from and with the villagers. In their minds and hearts, they carry with them the CBNRM framework, as one approach to participatory action research. In practical terms, students try very hard to:

1. Communicate with farmers and tell them about the existing resource situation.
2. Offer help to farmers, including giving ideas concerning ways to improve livelihoods and natural resource management, as and when it is possible since it is closely related to their research topic and participatory action research question.
3. Capture farmers' opinions as accurately as possible and incorporate some of these into their research design, so that their results might lead to more useful policy recommendations.
4. Construct a "platform" for improved communication between the community and outsiders, who are already executing or planning projects in the community, including government projects and projects funded by other donors, for example, through NGOs.
5. Discuss the situation with outside stakeholders to mobilize resources for local development.
6. Participate in a number of activities jointly developed by farmers and other local stakeholders.

This kind of commitment and effort, focusing on the sustainable development of rural communities, is seldom observed in other social science research in China. It is believed that it is giving students a solid basis for taking on rural development responsibilities in the future. As of January 2008, about 40% of the students who took part in the CBNRM courses, were working in development agencies and applying the CBNRM approach in their daily work. An in-depth tracer study is being conducted to assess the impact of our efforts on their work and on local people and environments. Evidence of the impact of student's research efforts is offered in the following pages.

Changes in farmers' livelihoods

Some farmers eagerly accepted resources and ideas from the students and, as a result, have been able to improve their livelihoods and capital assets in a variety of ways.

Case 1: Strengthening farmers' marketing intelligence

A Ph.D. student from COHD and an M.Sc. student from JLAU are doing their thesis research together in the same village, Zhangjiacun, in Jilin province. The Ph.D. thesis topic concerns networking in a rural community and the M.Sc. thesis topic is about changes in farmers' behaviour regarding adoption and adaptation of technologies.

After the students had worked in the community for a month, the farmers knew more about information sources and technologies and they started using this new knowledge to explore better marketing venues for their pigs. With the help of the two students, the farmers set up a computer in one of the villagers' homes and regularly obtained information about the pig market. They noted that from May to October 2007, although prices showed an upward trend, there were also strong fluctuations which made it difficult to make sound decisions about selling. However, with Internet access and constant monitoring of market information, the villagers managed to get good prices – about 0.2 yuan higher than average. They sold 320 pigs over a 5-month period and obtained about 16 000 yuan (about US $ 2340) above the average market price.

Thus, in the process, villagers enhanced their social and physical assets. They communicated more frequently among themselves, sharing knowledge and experience. By communicating with the students, they also had the opportunity to contact JLAU and the county agricultural bureau, which gave them access to practical knowledge about pig farming and related issues. This has allowed them to extend their network to other pig-raising farmers around China.

Case 2: Addressing women's needs with micro-credit

Another COHD Ph.D. student, whose thesis topic was farmers' use of financial resources and rural finance, is staying in the village of Shajiqu in Yanchi County, Ningxia Hui Autonomous Region. He helped the formers in road building and was quickly accepted as a friend.

A micro-credit project was going on in the village, but the student discovered that the women villagers were not very clear about how the project worked. During interviews with farmers, the student not only asked questions, but also tried to answer questions from the women about the micro-credit initiative. As a result, the number of women applying for credit doubled from 18 to 36, with the average loan about 2000 yuan (about US $ 290). Based on the average profit of clients of the micro-credit scheme, each of the 18 additional women could possibly increase her family income by about 350 yuan.

Changes in natural resource management

Students have observed that sometimes farmers do not know about methods to make their agricultural production more environmental friendly. For a long time, farmers have been encouraged by the government or the market to do things in a certain way, but now they are expected to make informed choices to redress land and water degradation and in purchasing appropriate inputs (types and quantities). In their interactions with farmers, the students emphasize the importance of obtaining broader market information and learning about research results and assistance for farmers, in terms of solving environmental problems. By facilitating information transfer, students are helping farmers start managing their natural resources effectively.

Case 3: On stage and in the field
Two COHD Ph.D. students are doing their thesis research in the village of Niu'anying in Guizhou province. One student's topic is policy intervention and livelihood change; the other is trying to identify the factors influencing adoption of a participatory approach. A third COHD student is doing M.Sc. thesis research on managing irrigation water in the same area.

The students have taken part in many village and township activities ever since they arrived. For example, the M.Sc. student helped at a cultural event organized by the township, where most villagers sang or danced – as did the two Ph.D. Students (Role playing during the CBNRM course came in very handy). On holidays, the three students developed interest amongst children in helping them with their fieldwork, and some of the children assisted with translation. The three students became very involved in village activities and are now considered members of the community.

During their interviews with farmers, the students found that the maintenance and use of local varieties of maize and rice are of concern. With the farmers, they discussed the advantages of local varieties compared with hybrids; for example, the local varieties are more drought-, disease-, and pest-resistant and require less water and pesticides. As a result of these discussions, about twenty farmers are preparing to plant and experiment with local varieties next year.

Case 4: Saving water and farmer-to-farmer exchanges
The JLAU student, mentioned in Case 1, together with research partners of JLAU, introduced water-saving techniques for the village irrigation system. Most (80%) of the villagers applied these methods and now use an average of 30% less water than before. One of the research partners, the Shuangyang County Agricultural Bureau, publicized the results locally. Leaders from twenty villages in Qijiazhen visited the village of Zhangjiacun in 2007 to see the water-saving experiment and they are now planning exchanges to learn the new technology.

Changes in the approach to managing community development

Some communities have small funds saved collectively or obtained from outside. After communications with students, villagers have started to consider new options for distributing the funds to finance village activities. Although it is not possible to assess the effect of this in terms of local development, there is evidence that villagers are creating more opportunities to mobilize resources that will benefit their communities.

Case 5: From individual to collective action

A COHD M.Sc. student (who graduated in 2007) for her thesis research compared the management and use of a community development fund in the village of Kutuan in Yanchi County, Ningxia, under autonomous village management with management supported by HOPE, a local NGO. Previously, villagers used to distribute their collective fund, which comes from rent on oil wells, to each individual household.

Through focus group discussions and interviews with each household, the student collected information – ideas and opinions – that farmers could not express frankly to "outsiders." The student summarized this information and provided the main findings to HOPE and other relevant stakeholders, such as the county forestry bureau.

Based on sound suggestions from farmers, the village obtained additional support from the government programme "Converting Cropping Land to Forest" and used its fund for trees to plant around the grasslands and in front of every farmer's house, following a collectively designed plan.

Case 6: Coping with tough policy measures

In addition to farmers' financial concerns, the Ph.D. student mentioned in Case 2 realized that the community had other socioeconomic and political issues. He not only adjusted his research design to investigate this broader (and more complex) picture, but also tried to do something for the farmers.

He took part in the community development planning process and introduced some tools – such as SWOT analysis (strengths, weaknesses, opportunities, threats) – that the farmers could use to analyse their own problems. He also expressed his opinion about villagers' priority activities, based on his knowledge of the marketing situation for their agricultural produce and the national policy context, specifically the so-called "forbidden grazing" policy.

Informed by previous research results, which clearly indicated that farmers are facing great difficulties coping with the grazing ban, and realizing that the policy could not be changed anytime soon, the student suggested that local people find a more positive strategy to cope, rather than the "furtive" grazing practices they were relying on. A proposal was put forward that one villager try to raise sheep using fodder. If this produced better benefits, this practice could be integrated into the village plan.

Changes in self-organizing capacities of farmers and communities

Farmers usually engage in cooperation in terms of production, marketing, cultural activities, etc. With students joining these activities and with more communication and exchanges, farmers have started to organize themselves in new ways – to deal with common problems, for example, by looking for solutions together.

Case 7: Making new connections with the outside world
The thesis topic of a COHD Ph.D. student is related to farmers' participation in development innovations in the village of Shanshengtai, Wuchuan County, Inner Mongolia. Based on discussions with members of the local potato association, she identified access to reliable market information as a key challenge. To help, she used funds from her fieldwork budget to help the association gain Internet access.

In addition, some of the association members, accompanied by the student, called experts to ask for advice directly – something they had never dared before. The association is now very active and has frequent contact with staff from the county government, agricultural bureau, Inner Mongolian Academy of Agricultural Sciences, and several companies. Through these contacts, the farmers have made use of increased resources from outside the community.

Case 8: Establishing new local organizations
Zhangjiacan in Jilin province (Case 1) now has a pig-raising association and a rice-planting interest group. It took time for the farmers to organize these groups. When the JLAU student first came to the community (after completing a PRD course), she realized that the farmers were interested in organizing, but were afraid to do so. Taking the opportunity to do her thesis research in the same village where she had done her PRD fieldwork, the student began by circulating technical information, then brought farmers together to discuss relevant questions. Over some time, the farmers became more

confident about organizing themselves and finding ways to adapt to "outside" requirements, including the market.

Case 9: Unafraid to tackle difficult issues through conflict mediation: In the village in Guizhou where the three students from Case 3 were staying, there were conflicts among the villagers; which could not be solved despite the villagers intervention. According to the villagers, the previous leader's corrupt practices were making them distrust the new village leader. When the students went to the village for their fieldwork and got to know the villagers well, they heard about this situation, and several other internal conflicts, and about the inappropriate use of the village development fund. The students met with various groups to learn more about these difficulties and were able to organise the villagers to jointly analyze the conflicts. Although the conflicts were not solved immediately, the villagers agreed to change how they used the development fund based on mutual decision-making. At the same time, they agreed to interact more with the new village leader as a way to build trust.

Learning from each other

Local partners are learning from these efforts as learning is taking place in terms of professional development, improved practice (informed by "theory"), and teamwork. Joint efforts are leading to more policy and financial support for community-based, participatory approaches. The key examples so far are in Ningxia and Guangxi, two of the three sites that have served as home bases for the CBNRM course. Support is allowing more local action, including experimentation, farmer organization, and better delivery of services, which, together, are contributing to improved livelihoods. The following stories illustrate the perspective of local partners in Guangxi and Ningxia on the contribution of the CBNRM efforts to local rural development.

Reflections on my participation in CBNRM curriculum development

by Long Zhipu, director, HOPE, Ningxia

Updating our knowledge is a necessity to understand the complexity of human interactions and to solve complicated social problems. We need multidisciplinary knowledge. The pity of this situation is that the development of the potential human resources has been limited by the narrow viewpoint that results from a discipline-oriented education system. In addition, although most of the students studying in the university are excellent, some of them could not adapt to the needs of working society after graduation. This CBNRM course is an innovation in teaching.

First, the teaching method is good. There is no longer a difference between teachers and students. In an environment of equity, everyone involved thinks about and discusses problems, contributing their own thinking and ideas and benefiting from others' ideas simultaneously. Participants enrich their own knowledge through this kind of open and interactive teaching process. Most important, one learns to identify and think about problems through a process of active participation, and learns how to study and solve problems in rural realities. This method of teaching is needed not only in the universities, but also in other training courses.

Second, the courses are designed with a focus on the integration of multidisciplinary knowledge and various perspectives, which is necessary for students who will be facing complicated social issues in the future. Furthermore, the course includes significant fieldwork, which facilitates problem-oriented learning and research through action. This focuses more on improving participants' synthesis capacities. And the interests of participants are stimulated when they study real demand emerging from a genuine rural situation.

Finally, participating in this course is also helpful for the institute, which is an NGO focusing on rural communities. Previously, the emphasis was on how to enhance resource management and how to improve the efficiency of resource use. But after participating in the CBNRM course, it was realized that although the resources themselves are very important, the development of management principles – by the community and by community members – is more important. The focus of our current work is on 10 selected communities with different characteristics to practice this new approach. It is expected to help those communities go further through various long-term interventions and, thus, provide examples to other communities in poor areas. However, the work is slow and the communities face many different problems and are made up of different groups and individuals. The participatory ideas that we learned in the course are needed to brainstorm and mobilize more resources and generate better ideas to solve the problems being faced using more integrated perspectives.

The curriculum development process gave a chance to reflect on the work and to learn a lot from the experiences of other partner institutes. Being an NGO with a commonwealth mission, our institute needs this kind of course and we also need students trained in this type of course.

A CBNRM story from Guangxi

by Jingsong Li, Centre for Chinese Agricultural Policy, Beijing, and Nanning, Guangxi

The Guangxi Participatory Plant Breeding (PPB) project has been involved in the CBNRM course at CAU since 2005. Each year, we presented our case study in the classroom to show students how action research takes shape in the field. When students came to our project villages, they visited farmers, observed their conditions, and tried to obtain information related to their research questions. Each year, the students focused on two topics – local governance system and farmers' livelihood. During 3–4 days in the field, the students collected information and analyzed their findings; this was useful to them, as well as useful to our project.

We have gained many insights by working with the CBNRM students. For example, during the 2005 course, the students found that there was a big gap between the county level and the township level extension services, and information and services could not be delivered directly from the county to the township. This important finding contributed to the development and implementation of our extension reform action research project. In 2006, the students used the "sustainable livelihood framework" to analyze PPB-related stakeholders in our project, especially the farmers, and based on their work we started rethinking the farmers' roles and their motivation for joining the PPB activities. In the 2007 course, some students discovered potential problems in how the village development fund was managed by the local farmer group. They made a kind of diagnosis of the fund, and their findings will be very helpful for future improvement.

So far, four CAU students (two M.Sc. and two Ph.D. candidates) have chosen our project sites for their thesis fieldwork after finishing the CBNRM course. During this fieldwork, they lived in the villages and made friends with local farmers. "We feel that they look like our children. We are even closer to them than our own children," one of the farmers said. The students discussed local livelihood strategies with people and in one case helped farmers decide to experiment with several varieties of cassava. Such activities connect the students with real rural life and, in the process, they have learned what action research is.

In addition to encouraging the project team, the students' field visits also "cheered up" local farmers and communities. As one farmer remarked, "We are happy when students come, because we feel that they care about us." The farmers always give a warm welcome to the students, prepare food, talk with them and answer their questions. In 2006, farmers even prepared a traditional cultural performance to show their hospitality. The last day of each field visit is always unforgettable, as the students present their findings and farmers share their stories.

Before leaving, students always contribute something to the local village development fund to support local development. One year, they helped bring electricity to the village office. The students needed the office as a base for interviewing farmers who are busy during the day and only have time to talk to the students in the evening. With lighting, the students can not only use the office, but the villagers also have a place to go to talk about collective activities.

I feel very lucky to be a facilitator for the CBNRM course. I have learned a lot from the curriculum development process, and discussions with colleagues and students always brought me deeper reflections on what we have done. The first thing I have learned is how a curriculum can be developed from initial ideas to a real course, especially if it opens the space for improvement. Each year, around the course, there will be at least two workshops – a planning workshop and one for conclusions and evaluation. The workshops always give the opportunity to the facilitators and students to address their fresh feedback. Secondly, the students' visit can bring some shining ideas for research and reflection. Lastly, I myself learned facilitating skills during the course process; it was a pleasant and fruitful time. In this CBNRM group, people learn from each other and some of us become friends.

Zhang Li (see her story earlier in the chapter) began her research by dealing with the problems of the rural extension system in a local village in Guangxi province as well. Her research is now contributing to local village development and reform of the extension system, making it more farmer focused. But doing research is more than just asking many questions and making observations. Here are some of the everyday experiences that are part of rural life.

A journey full of emotion (Part 2): my days in the villages

by Zhang Li

For my Ph.D. thesis research, I selected two villages in a county in Guangxi province as my fieldwork sites.

Who hindered the transfer of information?

In a focus group discussion in Qiaoli, one of the two villages where I stayed, farmers talked about signs of land degradation. They said that it has become harder and harder to grow maize, but they do not know why. They have been troubled by this problem for more than a year. I asked why they did not consult the extensionists. They answered that they thought the extensionists did not know the reasons either.

I knew that the county agricultural bureau has a device to test the soil quality. Thus, I facilitated a contact with the bureau so that the farmers could test their soils. The results indicated a fertility deficiency (due to poor fertilizing practices). To address the problem, the farmers decided to change their production practice to multiple cropping and applying more manure. Farmers had found an answer, and it seemed easy to guide them to it.

The fact that the thought of what looked like an easy thing (just going to county agricultural bureau and requesting a soil test), was so difficult for farmers, confused me. Why had they not found an answer in over a year? Who or what was hindering the transfer of information? By talking more with the farmers, I found out that communication between farmers and extensionists was very limited. They did not understand or trust each other. Farmers did not know what new services existed in the extension service centres or even what kind of services existed previously ... I concluded that things ought to be done to change this.

Finding the way together

Working together as a team with farmers, extensionists, policymakers, and researchers, we tried to find a way to change the situation. We decided on a participatory action approach, putting farmers first. Through a social learning process, all stakeholders discovered a new way of doing things, different from the past:

According to one farmer, "Now they pay attention to our needs ... and I have more chance to ask questions to the researchers and extensionists"; an extensionist remarked, "We are welcomed by farmers"; and one of the researchers explained, "I have learned a lot from the farmers."

Today, researchers and extensionists use participatory methods to understand farmers' needs and the extent of farmer satisfaction is now one of the indicators in their performance evaluation system. At the same time, policymakers agree that it is a good way to reform the extension system, and a new extension policy reform experiment is underway. It started in September 2007 and already covers villages in two townships. According to a follow-up survey, farmers appreciate the change.

Although it is only the beginning, our new way of working together, learning from each other and from the process, as well as reflecting on it, is helping us (the whole team) to find a way to adapt together.

Unforgettable days

The days in the Guangxi villages are unforgettable, because of the people and their stories.

The talkative, deaf grandpa – The grandpa of the family I lived with was deaf. His granddaughter told me, "My grandpa was very sorry, he said he did not talk to you these two days, because he was deaf." From the girl, I learned that the grandfather was once a village teacher. He had only been deaf for two years. From then on, I initiated talk with him, using paper and pencil. I discovered that he could even speak a little English, which he learned by himself. He turned out to be a talkative man.

Two young village teachers – One evening, the girl told me that two of her friends would come to visit me. They were young village teachers, and I was happy to meet them as there were few young people in the village; most of them have migrated. It turned out the teachers were as curious about me as I was about them. It was a difficult evening for me. They asked me a lot of questions – "What do you think about the nature of the Japanese people?" "What are the new policies for agriculture?" "In which place are farmers the richest?" They inquired about issues from the international to the local level, and I could see they yearned for the outside world and more information on how to give farmers a better life. I tried my best to answer all their questions, but my information and knowledge were limited. When I was back in Beijing, I bought some books and magazines and mailed them to the teachers. I could not think of anything else that I could do for them.

"One pair of trousers for a whole family" – There are several poor families in the village. One day, after I visited one of these households, the guide told me that the family was so poor that they had to wear one pair of trousers. The family consisted of a father and his three young sons. Their mother left them because of extreme poverty. In the village, this kind of single-parent family was quite common. Moved by this visit, I encouraged my younger "brothers and sisters" (student friends) to donate their clothes to the local poor. I was hopeful that from now on, the family would have more than one pair of trousers to wear.

My heart was heavy with these stories since I returned to Beijing for a short break from my fieldwork. There are different kinds of people living in rural areas, with multiple kinds of problems. I hope that more and more people will join in the complicated process of rural development, of working together with the local people to improve their livelihoods and their lives.

It is believed that good progress have been made in developing and strengthening the core capacities that are identified to be developed at both individual and organizational levels. These capacities are:

1. The ability to work together with community members and other stakeholders, with a focus on the attitudes, knowledge, and skills needed to decide how to facilitate the planning, experimentation, and assessment of CBNRM research and development initiatives.
2. The knowledge, attitudes, and skills needed to apply participatory action research in practice (in stakeholder analysis, consultation and planning, experimentation, and monitoring and evaluation).
3. The ability to express clear views about participatory action research, to link these views to field practices, and to communicate effectively about the development outcomes and impacts.
4. The ability to identify locally appropriate, effective individual and organizational capacity-building strategies.
5. The ability to apply a participatory curriculum development approach to reform the current teaching programmes and related research activities.

6. The knowledge and skills to manage participatory action research, teaching, training, and extension for CBNRM at the organizational level.

Conclusions

So far, the CBNRM mainstreaming process, although still in its early stages, has been an enriching experience for all those who are involved. It has demanded great labour and time till now, but since the initial steps have been taken, the intensity is expected to lessen over time. Careful preparation, a strong team, clear and shared goals, good technical and financial support, ongoing and systematic monitoring, involving students as much as possible, and continuous focus on learning-by-doing have been important in keeping things going on track.

The efforts are believed to have great merit as a means to increase significantly the relevance and effectiveness of natural resource management and rural development studies in China and as a means to reform China's higher education policy. The course and related activities that are being developed have set the stage for more profound teaching, research, and learning changes at COHD, at the M.Sc. and Ph.D. Programmes level, and indirectly, also at the B.Sc. level. Yang Huan (a 2006 CBNRM course assistant) speaks for many:

> First, the course is closely related to reality. The lack of awareness of reality, especially of rural areas, is a common disadvantage of our generation. We were trained as study machines to some extent. We have no chance to get to know society by experiencing it. Before we came to university and discovered this area of study, most of us knew nothing about rural life. So there is a big gap between theory and reality for students. It is hard for us to fill the gap if we lack the experience of living the life of farmers. This course gives us the chance to work in the field and see the life of farmers. For me, the facilitators' enthusiasm, experience, and achievements enlightened me. They give us examples and ways of thinking. The rest we did ourselves.

The course working groups and the fellowship support teams have been central in the work done so far. The tow factors of our sources are – bringing together an interdisciplinary team of colleagues from various organizations and involving a large number of students. A collective identity ("the CBNRM family") is there, and the set of methods that have been developed to tie activities, people, and objects together have all the features of a community of practice as described by Wenger. (1998; see also Wenger et al. 2002)

The experience suggests that the whole process of conceiving, designing, and delivering the course not only put curriculum reform into practice, but also contributed to changing organizational practices at COHD (and CAU). Many new relationships have developed and these have led to new initiatives. For example, a small group of students is taking on a review of all courses at COHD; the students, staff, and partners are jointly engaging in action research. This suggests that there is more to capacity development than narrowly defined skill or performance improvement and that curriculum development can actually be an expression of organizational change. Creating space for this type of change from within COHD seems to have benefited considerably from the support of partners in other organizations. How our efforts translate into organizational development, and how we can purposefully strengthen the process is yet to be analyzed.

Insights from learning, curriculum development, and rural development/CBNRM theories have served and will serve as guideposts, but practice tells us what works, and what does not, and where improvement can best be made. The introduction and systematic use of PM & E has been important; it keeps one's eyes and mind focused on learning about how to conduct the process – how to collaborate in a new, more effective and enjoyable way. All along, adjustments have been made and there has been an willingness to learn from mistakes and shortcomings. This openness helped in making many adjustments and, very likely, will result in more changes in the near future.

Ongoing critical reflection, not only to monitor courses and broader processes, but also to identity development, has been central. The experience with the exercises in the art of asking questions point to the challenge of paying more attention to the nature and practice of critical reflection. In their evaluation of the course, many students have mentioned their interest in becoming more skilled at asking questions – not only research questions but also questions about their learning in "school." We were surprised, and often moved, by the depth of their resolve. But not all students are the same; some are eager and able to manifest their learning experience, while others are quieter. A better eye for, understanding, and an approach to identity development and these differences could enrich the facilitation process and collaborative learning (Cranton 2006: 79–99, 135–157).

The relevance of CBNRM as a new speciality has been discovered, in relation to the many potentialities and problems embedded in the complex and rapidly changing rural realities in China. Central to this are connections with each other and with the people with whom the cooperation takes place in rural areas across the country. The efforts to integrate these realities into the very core of the courses create the curriculum effectively. As a result, the sense of the dynamic roles that rural development professionals can play in today's rapidly changing China has been sharpened. Box 13 offers a synthesis of the learning.

Box 13. Summary of the CBNRM mainstreaming approach

Vision

- Making a commitment to working together (mutual engagement), agreeing on shared goals.
- Defining do-able and practice-focused learning objectives and a longer-term horizon for achieving mainstreaming objectives.

Involvement and interaction

- Free and active participation of all participants, especially students.
- Involvement of students in management tasks (nurturing champions).
- New ways (horizontal communications and interactions) of working together and doing things differently as a way to put organizational change into practice.
- Dynamic and creative teaching and facilitation methods – fostering joint learning.

Approach

- CBNRM viewed as a holistic and dynamic approach to address real-life problems (although not easy to put into practice).
- Useful theory–practice links, although these could be strengthened, for example, in thesis work.
- Going into the field and learning by doing, largely self-directed, but together with local partners and guided by ongoing monitoring.
- CBNRM/comanagement/joint learning/teamwork – the course and other activities reflect CBNRM in real life.

Innovative use of participatory monitoring and evaluation

- Using PM & E – with a "light, useful and fun" approach – to track progress and make changes (direct use of results), deepen learning through ongoing reflection, raise awareness about learning process (participation and methods), a self-managed process.

Links

- Building strong support – political, technical, financial.
- Making strong connections with partners – this leads to synergies and is the key to innovation, i.e., new ideas, new practices.
- Responding to policy dynamics (the education reform that is underway).
- Creating communities of practice, which, in turn, help get the work done in effective and joyful ways; these communities have started to transfer results and lessons learned to other places.

Challenges

Looking ahead, challenges have been identified in four main areas – the courses and fellowship support programme, mainstreaming our efforts at CAU and JLAU, mainstreaming CBNRM in the higher education system at large, and influencing government and NGOs that employ rural development professionals.

In fine-tuning the courses and fellowship support programme, it is considered necessary to pay more attention to the use of conventional research methods, such as surveys, case studies, life stories/histories, and situational analysis and to integrate them into the work. There is also room to expand the role of the field visit part of the course – increasing preparation time and actual time in the field. Strengthening the skills of the facilitation group is envisioned by both staff and students to improve the quality of interactions among all participants and allow them to delve deeper into issues and questions that emerge.

Although good progress has been made, the road to mainstreaming CBNRM at CAU and JLAU is still a long one. Strengthening the links between the courses and M.Sc. and Ph.D. dissertation work and gain respect and support for CBNRM-oriented field research, including fair and appropriate examination or evaluation of theses and other research reports is what is wished for. Sharing the learning and bringing other facilitator-teachers and key decision-makers on board can be made better. Obtaining more financial support is also a priority. More staff are encouraged to do CBNRM-oriented field research.

There are opportunities to use participatory curriculum development approaches to improve other courses and develop new ones, as a contribution to building more coherent programmes in which, components interconnect. What is needed is to maintain and continuously rejuvenate the engaged and committed working groups that have the space to manoeuvre with flexibility and relative autonomy. This includes supporting new and younger "champions" of innovation.

The tasks are considerable in terms of mainstreaming the efforts in Chinese higher education at large. They include sharing good practices and encouraging their adaptation at other universities in an effective and efficient manner. Political and financial support from CAU, JLAU, and the Ministry of Education to achieve long-term sustainability is sought to obtain. Further development of an effective and useful approach to assessment of CBNRM mainstreaming outcomes and impacts of the efforts at large is wished for.

There is a need to connect with potential employers, in China and outside the country to imporve professional opportunities for graduates with CBNRM expertise. One way to do this is to involve them in the course from the very beginning. They could be invited to participate in one session or in the whole course, discuss opportunities for cooperative fieldwork (thesis work or other) and keep themselves informed about the initiative. At the same time, potential employers could be requested to provide information to students about job opportunities and special assignments.

Change comes about slowly, and requires a well-designed, but flexible strategy, that is embedded in – but not glued too strongly to – the practices of the organization or organizations taking part. Although it is still too early to fully assess the mainstreaming strategy, one can be confident about the good progress that has been made so far.

Comparing the cases. Case study analysis workshop in Beijing, China.
Photo: Ronnie Vernooy.

5

Comparing the Case Studies

Ronnie Vernooy, Maria Celeste H. Cadiz, Dindo Campilan, Qi Gubo, and Zhang Li

New constellations of learning

The three cases described in this book represent diverse but congruent, unfolding paths to learning – design, processes, and results. They include the development of holistic and dynamic curricula that integrate the various approaches and tools used in participatory CBNRM and PR & D research. The three initiatives offer curricula to different categories of learners – academics and graduate students; practitioners and researchers in the field; community groups; and policymakers. The three cases share the common feature of making curriculum development an emergent, collective, and adapative process, rather than establishment of a pre-set blueprint delivered by teachers or instructors who are the "know all" and "know best" and who are not truly engaged in the process.

The cases bring together the knowledge and expertise about CBNRM and PR & D of a diversity of people and organizations, working in a variety of political, socioeconomic and agro-ecological contexts. In all three cases, partners and participants have strengthened a number of important capacities – going beyond mere technical expertise, through a prolonged process of working and learning together. This pooling of expertise involves students, researchers, practitioners, community groups, policymakers, and staff of international organizations. Among those social actors are individuals who are either more or less experienced (in terms of dealing with rural development questions and being involved in capacity development processes), belonging to groups or organizations with often diverse histories. However, they are motivated to join forces to engage in experimentation and experience sharing.

The cases develop and use reflection effectively to increase the quality of the collaborative learning, including advocating CBNRM, PR & D, and participatory action research approaches to key organizational decision-makers and policymakers. This is done through the systematic integration of and experimentation with participatory monitoring and evaluation mechanisms from the very beginning. Advocacy and mainstreaming take place through a variety of means, including policy analysis, supporting peer-to-peer and community-to-community networking, linking communities with other development practitioners, and outreach efforts.

In this concluding chapter, an attempt to answer the original research questions has been made, identify similarities and differences among the cases, synthesize lessons learned, and point out challenges. The key concepts, methods, and practical considerations identified in the introduction that are related to learning at both individual and organizational levels are reviewed. The analysis in this chapter results from a joint effort of looking critically at the work, achievements, and unresolved or new questions. In the first part of the chapter, the main features of the cases are summarized in terms of whose, what, why, and how the capacities were developed. In the second part, the focus is on results, lessons learned, and challenges. The reflections are expected to deepen both the theory and practice of capacity development and collaborative learning.

Learning together

The PR & D programme (Chapter 2) reached out to a large and diverse number of organizations across South Asia (16 in all), including universities, NGOs, national agricultural research system members, and Consultative Group on International Agricultural Research centres. The interest to work in the field of natural resource management is common among these organization and the participants who took part in the programme – including research, training, education, and advocacy efforts – have a desire to strengthen social analysis skills and to integrate these into existing knowledge bases and experiences. Actual research done as part of the programme involved local partners. UPWARD, LI-BIRD, IDRC, and IFAD joined forces to lead the initiative, while UPWARD and LI-BIRD took care of most of the actual implementation.

The ALL in CBNRM programme (Chapter 3) has a strong practitioner focus, bringing together staff from government agencies, NGOs, and universities, many if not most of them engaged in CBNRM efforts ranging from research to development work, through programmes or projects at the local level. The programme combines capacity development and networking of people and their organizations, who are interested in participatory development approaches to rural development and CBNRM. Five organizations (UPWARD, IIRR, RECOFTC, CBCRM, UPLB) teamed up to lead and implement the programme, bringing together a rich and diverse basis of knowledge and experience. Numbers and levels of participation changed, as could be predicted, but the span of the programme has remained broad.

In China (Chapter 4), the CBNRM mainstreaming initiative focuses not only on postgraduate students and a few undergraduates, university staff (professors, teachers, researchers), and key policymakers in higher education (at universities and at the Ministry of Education), but also involves local partners (government and NGO staff and farmers) through the CBNRM and PRD (and similar) courses and through support for field research offered to students. Over the years, the number and diversity of partners have increased considerably, and continue to increase as students spread their wings and fly to other sites in the country, thus creating a large web of connections and interactions.

The three cases are all going beyond the "capacity builders" (i.e., all learners in the process) in the narrow sense of the term, i.e., they share a focus on real-life learning situations that involve rural communities and other stakeholders in natural resource management. The dynamics in which the learners are immersed mirror, to varying degrees, real-life natural resource management contexts, characterized by resource degradation (on the increase in most areas), competition and conflict (fuelled by shifting market interests, policy interventions, voluntary or forced migration, and the emergence of new civil society organizations), unpredictability and insecurity. In all three cases, facilitators are also an integral part of the learning process. They are no longer conventional teachers or trainers, but capacity builders and learners in their own right.

In the context of the increasing complex political, socioeconomic, and agro-ecological environments across Asia – expressed through increasingly serious natural resource management problems, seemingly more devastating natural disasters, and growing socioeconomic interdependencies on regional and global scales, are easier said than done. Designing and executing holistic and dynamic capacity strategies has become a complicated task which, requires ongoing adaptation to remain effective.

Box 14. The role of IDRC

The three initiatives have benefitted from the financial and technical support of IDRC and have developed close connections with the centre. An analysis of IDRC's role in their evolution revealed the following elements contributed through the involvement of IDRC programme officers in the three initiatives:

- Introduced the concept of centres of excellence for CBNRM, with a commitment to support their establishment together with interested partners.
- Brokered partnerships among individuals and organizations, in-country (e.g., China) and among countries (e.g., PR & D, ALL in CBNRM) to develop and effectively implement this series of initiatives.
- Catalyzed access to additional resources, with initial IDRC support attracting co-funding from other donors (i.e., PR & D).
- Provided guidance with enough leeway to allow for dynamic experimentation and innovation in collaborative learning.
- Showed interest and engaged actively in learning as a partner in the new capacity development efforts.
- Provided technical knowhow and inspiration based on IDRC experience.
- Facilitated the sharing of experiences, critical reflection on these experiences, and cross-case comparative analysis (such as in this book).

These multiple and mutually supportive contributions point to roles of a donor agency that go beyond the mere provision of funds. Underlying these is the high value IDRC places on capacity development – making it an integral part of its overall programme agenda and stimulating systematic learning about it.

However, an issue of concern is the duration of support, which, given IDRC's focus on a project timeframe, is normally relatively short

(3 years). (The China case is an exception, which benefits from an experimental five-year commitment.) A recommendation resulting from this, looking at the three cases, is to consider longer timelines, particularly for organizational capacity development or institutionalization. This would allow more prolonged and in-depth experimentation and more thorough assessment.

The more you invest the more you harvest: the capacities developed

Actual capacities developed in all three cases are based on real-life needs and demands, reflecting a holistic and dynamic approach to professional rural development work and life. Today's major natural resource management questions invariably concern situations in which various social actors with different interests and points of view operate, interact, and often debate and compete over resources. Meaningful and effective capacity development initiatives need to address this basic fact which the three cases have tried to do.

Although informed by theory, ranging from pedagogy to rural development sociology to ecology, key capacities developed are practice focused. The three cases emphasize that exercises in the classroom and in the field contribute to changes in attitude, knowledge, and skills, which, when combined, can be applied in everyday working conditions. This is a major departure from most conventional (academic) capacity development. All three cases address management capacities, which is another expression of a holistic and dynamic approach, while at the same time pointing to the issue of sustainability. Thus, the combined capacities to be developed are both an end and a means.

The PR & D programme defines core capacities as understanding, doing, and enabling PR & D. The programme links the strengthening of technical capacities to the development of appropriate values and norms supporting stakeholders' participation; it also tries to link individual with team or organizational capacities.

The ALL in CBNRM programme aims to develop and strengthen perspectives, principles, concepts, methods, and tools in participatory development organized in a logical framework. Perhaps more implicitly than the PR & D programme, ALL in CBNRM also envisions connecting individual with organizational capacity development, although a clear and coherent strategy or strategies seems to be missing.

In China, the aim is to develop and strengthen six key capacities which cover both individual and organizational dimensions. The focus on mainstreaming also has a strong policy dimension and, as such, implies the application of a learning-by-doing approach to influence policy agendas. China's Ministry of Education has made a strong effort to renew its higher education curriculum to be responsive to the rapid changes in the country, and the CBNRM mainstreaming initiative aims to directly inform and inspire this reform process.

Key capacities developed across the three cases are:

1. The ability to learn together and master social learning in the sense of becoming less individualistic and more humane.
2. The ability to work together, in a team or teams, with community members and other stakeholders, focusing on improving attitudes, knowledge, and skills, with particular attention to facilitation of the planning, experimentation, and assessment of CBNRM and participatory action research and development initiatives.
3. Recognition of the complexities with which biophysical and human elements interact in the processes of gaining access to, using, and managing resources, and how the outcomes of this interaction determine sustainability (or lack of sustainability).
4. The knowledge, attitudes, and skills to put participatory action research into *practice.*
5. The ability to express clear views about participatory action research and communicate effectively about development outcomes and impacts.
6. The ability to identify locally appropriate, effective individual and organizational capacity-building strategies.
7. The ability to apply a participatory curriculum development approach to reform the current teaching programmes and related research activities.

These capacities are well-defined, but together make up an ambitious agenda. The three cases point to the need for concerted and longer-term efforts to develop or strengthen them in a meaningful way. Operating within the current time horizon has proved to be a real challenge, in particular for the PR & D programme (which has effectively ended) and the ALL in CBNRM initiative (its future is uncertain). The China case has an initial five-year operational timeline, but this also seems very short in view of its goal of effective national policy reform.

Filling gaps, addressing challenges: learning rationales

On one hand, the three cases emerged to address perceived gaps, shortcomings, and challenges in conventional capacity development in the field of natural resource management. The cases are based on the premise that rural development should start and "end" with rural realities – so often not the case. On the other hand, the cases take a more positive stance, in the sense of being novel capacity development experiments, designed and developed through and by new configurations of cooperating professionals. As such, they are actual instances of experiential action learning and of the formation of new "communities of capacity development practice." Clearly, the three cases illustrate a desire to deepen their work and continue the learning – now in terms of putting in place a novel action research agenda applied to capacity development.

The PR & D programme emphasized the fact that holistic and dynamic natural resource management requires joint learning and action within and among communities and more than the dominant transfer-of-technology approach. The programme built on previous, dispersed and more individually oriented efforts, in some cases renewing past efforts, in others, starting afresh. As a regional programme, it faced the challenge of being able to operate in a diversity of institutional contexts, which was not always easy.

The ALL in CBNRM programme emerged from a need to improve current CBNRM practice. Based on an analysis of narratives of natural resource management projects and organizations in the region, the Programme set out to strengthen the practice of involving communities in capacity building in NRM and CBNRM, which is widely recognized as paramount for successful practice, but often poorly executed. The programme also aimed to build synergies among the numerous CBNRM "advocates" (often with different readings of CBNRM), covering a rich panoply of ecosystems and organizational contexts. The programme envisioned bringing this diversity of advocates together, creating a mutually enriching programme centred around the concept and practice of adaptive management.

In China, there was a strongly felt need among the pioneers of the CBNRM mainstreaming initiative to increase the relevance and effectiveness of rural development studies. The pioneers saw an opportunity to build on a decade of experience in the country and elsewhere, to mainstream CBNRM in education, rural development policies, extension, and research and, as already mentioned, to contribute to the higher education reform taking place in the country. The pioneers shared a vision and willingness to tread on these goals together even though this was not done before.

Learning through collective action: methods and tools

The PR & D programme defined its learning approach as integrated, grounded, interactive, continuous, and reflective. The methods included class-based training, field research, mentoring, review workshops, and the provision of information support services, including the use of the Worldwide Web (which did not prove as successful as expected).

The ALL in CBNRM programme used a so-called blended modality including face-to-face team discussions, regional workshops, online e-forums, practical experience, field mentoring, and small grants for research and to develop learning resources.

In China, learning takes place through multiple action–reflection cycles, in the classroom and in the field, informed by learning theories, participatory curriculum development, and participatory action research. The CBNRM mainstreaming theory of action has six interrelated components, including participatory curriculum development, supporting community-based, participatory rural development field-research practices, the support of champions, policy analysis and advocacy, PM & E, and teacher-to-teacher and student-to-student "extension."

The three cases have the following in common – an experiential and learner-focused approach, a diversity of methods, and a deliberate orientation toward practice. They depart radically from the conventional teacher-as-expert model. The three cases also share a focus on what could be called the meso-organizational level, both in terms of inputs or organizational/managerial set-up and outcomes, i.e., contributing to organizational change. They embody the concept of social learning in the sense of the capacity to learn together and becoming more social in our professional lives.

They make audacious use of PM & E, not only to assess results, but also to make adjustments along the road, in the true sense of reflective learning by doing. The cases experiment with a menu of methods, often novel, e.g., in China, the introduction of games, role plays, photography and video, and student peer review. In terms of management, they try practicing a form of shared leadership and facilitation, among the organizations involved, among the facilitators, and (in China) between the more experienced and the younger generations. Practice, through in-depth fieldwork is at the heart of the efforts. The three cases are characterized by a high degree of openness – facilitators do their best to act with open minds and hearts and to fully engage with learners in a process of joint discovery.

Based on previous experience showing the usefulness of designing and using PM & E from the very beginning, the three cases deliberately made PM & E part of the learning process for students, staff, and others, paying attention to both dynamics and results. The three cases experimented with combinations of self-assessment, reviews by mentors/facilitators/supervisors/local partners/peers, a diversity of tools including story telling, and the deliberate use of results during the whole learning process.

Changes observed

The changes brought about by the three initiatives are significant – they include strong individual achievements and organizational gains, mainly at the meso level. A number of interesting and some unexpected results emerged, which will be highlighted. In retrospect, these results are perhaps not so surprising, and they seem to speak about the quality of the efforts being made and still underway.

The PR & D programme increased PR & D capacity among individuals, their organizations, and partners; increased the use of PR & D in the work of organizations; gained greater support for PR & D from key decision-makers; and increased the allocation of organizations' resources for PR & D. As a result of the programme, there was an improvement in the participating organizations' attainment of goals. Many received recognition for their achievements and, in most cases, participants and their home organizations saw an increase in external support. The most striking result of the programme was the creation of a regional community of PR & D practitioners and a loose network of organizations interested in PR & D.

The ALL in CBNRM programme produced a variety of learning pathways [a term inspired by Paolo Freire (2000)], characterized by improved capacities in participatory development approaches to

CBNRM (e.g., the use of multistakeholder bases for action), increased social learning capacities, and some signs of transformative learning (increased confidence and more dynamic teamwork). The programme is also having a "ripple effect" on communities and local government officials. The coordinating partners have strengthened their development and participatory management and implementation skills and, are building a community of practice step-by-step, which is also emerging at national levels. The key results have been, first, the insight that effective and meaningful learning represents a true social process and, second, through the combined efforts of all, some policy changes are coming about.

The achievements in China have been remarkable. What started as a courageous effort by a small team of pioneers is now becoming a deeper and broader process of innovation, showing that changes can be brought about even in a strongly hierarchical and still centralized system. Attitudes, knowledge, skills, and practice of students, university staff, and other stakeholders (in terms of the key defined CBNRM capacities) are all undergoing dramatic change. Organizational changes at various universities and partner organization are also occurring. The China experience has inspired colleagues in other Asian countries as well, notably Vietnam, Laos, and Mongolia. Through IDRC and its partners (e.g., CAU), key results and insights are also finding their way to other regions.

In China, the most striking results are the transformative learning evident in students, the value added in the form of new social capita at the individual and organizational levels, ideas and insights finding their way into the field and policy levels, and the discovery that the capacity development process has become more and more like a CBNRM process in the field. The China experience, while continuing to evolve, is now starting to serve as an example for others. New theoretical insights are emerging, such as concerning the emergent nature of effective learning.

Box 15. Outputs of the programmes

The three programmes described in these case studies have developed diverse ways of producing outputs, several of which are experimental in nature – the Knowledge Bank developed by ALL in CBNRM, writing and the use of role playing in China. All three cases have given very high priority to documenting their approach, processes, and achievements as means for critical self-reflection and sharing. Outputs are contributing in varying degrees, to the development of an identity by the emerging communities of practice.

The PR & D programme produced a series of papers presented at seminars and conferences, in-house training materials, a database of PR & D information resources, and one book. The ALL in CBNRM programme has a website, a Knowledge Bank, multiple resources developed by learning groups, presentations, programme briefs, fact sheets, a programme booklet, a CD with video, and a brochure. Teams at the various universities in China have produced (and continue to update on a yearly basis) teaching materials, briefs, posters, photography exhibits, brochures, and websites (at CAU and JLAU); together, partners have published one scientific article (in the *Journal of Agricultural Education and Extension*) and two books (with another in press).

Lessons and possible explanations

Each of the cases generated some important lessons, some of them specific to the case, but several relevant to all three cases.

Based on the principle of cyclical action–reflection, collaborative learning design can be very effective when it employs participatory action approaches anchored in rural realities. To facilitate learning at both the individual and organizational levels, there is a need for a variety of learning methods appropriately blended to maximize advantages and offset weaknesses. These methods include face-to-face discussion, e-forum-facilitated discussion, reading of supplementary materials, group discussion with resource persons, fieldwork, backstopping and mentoring, provision and guided production of knowledge resources, small research grants, and workshops. A community of practice can be an effective means to mobilize the expertise required to design and implement appropriate mixes of methods, but it does not get established by decree.

The PR & D programme, as assessed in light of its own "theory of action," learned that the following factors contributed to success – an emphasis on sustained learning processes rather than one-time events; a direct link between classroom learning and immersion in field action; customized learning support through flexible group learning, monitoring, and demand-driven information services; joint contributions and benefits rather than one-way, dole-out investments; and PR & D as facilitative capacity to complement (not substitute for) other research capacities. No one of these factors contributed to the programme's achievements, but rather their combination and interplay.

The ALL in CBNRM programme observed the importance of various modalities in learning facilitation; the need to support experiential learning through grants for research and the development of field-based resources; and the value of face-to-face interaction, mentoring, and regional exchange. Reflecting on the whole process, it is becoming clear that effective learning for CBNRM means true social learning, because adaptation (the desired outcome of the learning) is fundamentally a social process. In other words, for capacity development efforts to be effective, expected outcomes need to be mirrored in the learning process itself, not just viewed as the "final" product.

The China team summarized its main lessons as:

1. Obtain strong policy support, as this is crucial to allow audacious experimentation.
2. Careful preparation is half the work, and this includes team building (a never-ending process) and the identification of clear learning objectives leading to doable results.
3. Use an inclusive, participatory, step-wise process in time and in space.
4. Build on strong field experience, characterized by interactions with diverse partners, contrasting sites, and challenging CBNRM issues.
5. Use PM & E from the start and throughout the process.
6. Rely on students and nurture champions. Surprisingly, strong identity development emerged with features of transformative learning – giving shape to the notion that any good curriculum is itself an emerging property, rather than a product to be delivered.

Several common lessons were revealed, each of which could be useful to deepen both practical and theoretical insights:

1. Good design principles include combining instrumental, communicative, and transformative learning elements; the integration of key learning objectives into both content and process; the use of PM & E from the start; the appropriate use of mentoring; and dynamic and shared facilitation.
2. Partnership building has a central role, starting from mutual engagement and commitment to a shared agenda, and full

acknowledgment of the politics involved. Third parties can play a useful role of a broker in bringing together organizations that previously saw themselves as competitors or that did not discern any common interest in exploring partnerships for capacity development. In the PR & D case, UPWARD played a similar role; in the other two cases, IDRC assumed this role to varying degrees.

3. An integrated but adaptive design process is valuable – including a mind and heart open to unexpected results and allowing for adjustments. Learning pathways, similar to professional or personal pathways, tend to unfold rather than being simple, linear, or causal.
4. "Grounded" learning is a necessary base and end point; thus, full engagement with real life situations, marked by the multiple realities of the participants in capacity development, is crucial.
5. There is a fundamental need to master social learning, i.e., how to connect, engage, and work together, respect and deal with different learning styles and pathways.
6. High-quality results follow from mutual investment and team efforts, but this process requires time, energy, and guidance. There is simply no blueprint for capacity development in the field of CBNRM, which is changing all the time, and becoming more complex.
7. Identity development is powerful as it seems to "feed" or support the development or strengthening of more technical capacities. The emergence of this result seems to indicate the usefulness of a holistic but dynamic learning strategy [for a more detailed discussion of this feature, see the results of a recent tracer study among participants of the CBNRM mainstreaming initiative (Zhang Li 2008)].
8. Redefining professional relevance (by students, staff, policymakers, and farmers) in a rapidly changing world is challenging, leading to the difficult task of designing, continuously reassessing, and adjusting learning strategies.
9. Policy support is needed from the start. Such support can be generated within organizations (e.g., at the level of a department or college), among organizations (formal or informal agreements to cooperate), or at a sectoral or multisectoral level (e.g., a ministry of education).

Challenges encountered and moving ahead

The three programmes have encountered a number of challenges, which are common to all three, notwithstanding the progress and achievements to date.

The programmes still operate within a largely conventional capacity development system and financial contributions from national systems remain limited. Bringing about change requires long-term horizons, and often people and resources are limited and in constant flux. It takes time and effort to mobilize leadership support for the kinds of efforts embodied in the three cases, given their experimental, complex, and "radical" nature. It also takes time and effort and a lot of courage to develop adequate facilitation skills and to find opportunities to practice. Team-building requires major time and effort, as well as pioneers.

Capacity development schedules and dynamics, when tied to project funding and administrative requirements, do not always fully harmonize with time cycles of farmers and their crops.

Aiming for organizational change requires addressing policy issues, which is always difficult. Rural development in the countries where the programmes operate remains a relatively low priority in terms of policy change. Demand for rural development professionals remains uncertain and, in general, seems to be moving "against the flow" of the job market.

The PR & D programme discovered that much more time was required in moving from individual to organizational capacity development, for example, to build a critical mass of PR & D advocates and to fully involve the heads of the organizations. The programme also had to face the "temporary" nature of employment of many PR & D practitioners, who are tied to projects or programmes, which directly affects sustainability and scaling-up efforts. At present, in South Asia, organizations focusing on rural development seem to be constrained by financial resources, which often leads to a lower priority on capacity development efforts in general, and PR & D in particular.

The ALL in CBNRM programme's major challenges include finding the most effective way to refine the programme modalities and facilitation methods; improve the collaborative management partnership; sustain the programme and its benefits through strategic alliances; and use the programme outputs and outcomes to influence policy.

In China, both students and staff are faced with a conflict between personal interests and the requirements imposed by the wider organizational context, i.e., students are often not free to do the kind of fieldwork they like, but must meet the demands of their supervisors and other staff. Organizational change is slow because of the hierarchical nature of the education system and the many rules and regulations concerning curriculum development, administration, and supervision. At the policy level, the interest in high-tech-oriented education programmes continues to increase, which is also evident at the university level.

Enabling and supporting factors

Reviewing the cases together, it was identified that a number of key factors enabled or supported CBNRM capacity development efforts and CBNRM mainstreaming. These factors can be organized into the central elements of a learning strategy or theory of action and, as such, can best be viewed as factors that need to be "produced" or mobilized strategically. These insights are offered as a conclusion to this book and, hopefully it inspires and guides others.

Vision: At the heart of any sound strategy is a strong commitment to work together, to engage fully, combined with an agreement on shared goals. Defining doable learning objectives (which can be adjusted over time) and a longer-term horizon for achieving mainstreaming objectives are the other key ingredients in an inspiring vision.

Involvement and interaction: A dynamic strategy requires free and active participation, particularly of students in the case of higher education contexts. The involvement of students in management tasks is a powerful way to nurture "champions." Novel ways of working together – horizontal communications and interactions – and doing things differently (as a way to put organizational change into practice) supported by dynamic and creative teaching/facilitation methods will foster joint learning and create synergy.

Co-ownership: Sharing responsibilities, efforts, and the fruit of the work can create a strong basis for long-term achievements. It is important to recognize that contributions can take many forms, ranging from material to spiritual. Mutual willingness to accept contributions relative to partner's pool of resources is perhaps the key to effective ownership.

Approach: CBNRM, seen as a holistic and dynamic approach to address real-life rural livelihoods problems, continues to be relevant in Asia, although the approach is not easy to put into practice. Creating theory–practice links is central to CBNRM capacity development – going out into the field and learning by doing, together with local partners who are the frontline workers, experiencing the rapid changes taking place firsthand. The more the learning strategy mirrors CBNRM in practice, the more likely the results will be fruitful.

Innovative use of PM & E: PM & E based on a "light, useful, and fun" approach greatly helps track progress and make changes, while also deepening the learning-through-ongoing-reflection process, including learning about the learning process itself.

Linkages: Organizational change ought not to be construed and pursued as the end result, but achieved by building strong supportive relationships. This starts with the partners and participants who are directly involved and spreads from them to others. Linkages may have political, technical, and financial elements. Strong connections with partners take time to develop, but, once established, can create synergies. New connections are the source of innovation, i.e., new ideas, new practices. Emerging communities of practice, in turn, facilitate the work in an effective way.

These enabling factors must be constructed during the process; they cannot be found somewhere and applied. In this sense, from the hearts of the three cases the actual meaning of *toward* centres of excellence has emerged.

As Qi Gubo summarized it in her story (Chapter 4):

> I have learned a lot about the spiral-up process of awareness raising and behavioural change. This process is like a long road of change, in terms of discovering the theoretical contributions that action research can make, reconciling the conflict between short-term thesis research and longer-term action research, linking knowledge accumulation with practice, complementing different methodologies and teaching methods, acknowledging fully the roles of local communities and local people, and accepting everybody and believing in the potential contribution of everybody, including those who at the beginning do not show much active interest.

References

ALL in CBNRM. 2008. Evaluation and planning workshop: highlights of the workshop. Regional Community Forestry Training Center for Asia and the Pacific, Bangkok, Thailand.

Armitage, D.; Berkes, F.; Doubleday, N., ed. 2007. *Adaptive Co-Management: Collaboration, Learning, and Multi-Level Governance*. University of British Columbia Press, Vancouver, BC, Canada.

Baser, H.; Morgan, P. 2008. *Capacity, Change and Performance*. European Centre for Development Policy Management, Maastricht, Netherlands. Discussion paper 59B. Available: siteresources.worldbank.org/INTCDRC/Resources/CapacityChangePerformanceReport.pdf (accessed 6 Oct. 2008).

Bessette, G. 2003. *Isang Bagsak*: a *Capacity Building and Networking Programme in Participatory Development Communication*. International Development Research Centre, Ottawa, Canada.

Bessette, G. 2004. *Involving the Community: A Guide to Participatory Development Communication*. International Development Research Centre, Ottawa, ON, Canada, and Southbound, Penang, Malaysia. Available: www.idrc.ca/en/ev-52226-201-1-DO_TOPIC.html (accessed 13 Sept. 2008).

Bessette, G.; Vernooy, R. 2005. 'Strengthening Individual and Organizational Capacities for CBNRM: towards CBNRM Centers of Excellence (a concept paper)'. International Development Research Centre, Ottawa, ON, Canada. Available: www.idrc.ca/fr/ev-81766-201-1-DO_TOPIC.html (accessed 13 Sept. 2008).

Bessette, G.; Vernooy, R.; Zhang Li. 2008. 'Strengthening Organizational Capacity Development: the Centres of Excellence in CBNRM in Asia initiative'. Paper prepared for the ENRM Annual Learning Forum 2008. International Development Research Centre, Ottawa, ON, Canada. Unpublished.

Cadiz, M.C.H. 2005. 'Communication for empowerment: The practice of participatory communication in development'. In Hemer, O.; Tufte, T. ed. 2005. *Media and Global Change: Rethinking Communication for Development*. CLASCO, Buenos Aires, Argentina and Nordicom, Göteborg, Sweden. pp. 123–144.

Cadiz, M.C.H.; Caballero, L.M.A. 2006. 'Isang Bagsak South-East Asia: Towards institutionalizing a Capacity-building and Networking Programme in Participatory Development Communication for Natural Resource Management'. In Besette, G. ed. *People, Land, and Water:*

Participatory Development Communication for Natural Resource Management. Earthscan, London, UK, and International Development Research Centre, Ottawa, Canada. Available: www.idrc.ca/en/ev-105009-201-1-DO_TOPIC.html (accessed 13 Nov. 2008).

Campilan, D.; Bertuso, A.; Ariyabandu, R.; Sister, L. ed. 2006. *Learning Participation in Action: Field Research Experiences in South Asia*. CIP-UPWARD, Los Baños, Laguna, Philippines. p. 198 pp. Available: www.cip-upward.org/main/AMC/snapins/DOC/DOC_DocumentsViewer.asp?DocID=1143 (accessed 25 Sept. 2008).

Campilan, D.; Perez, J.C.; Sim, J.M.; Boncodin, R.M. 2003. 'Evaluating Organizational Capacity in Participatory Research: the Case of NPRCRTC'. *BSU Research Journal* 29: 1–35.

Castillo, G.; Campilan, D. 1999. 'Nurturing a Network: Lessons in the Evolution of the UPWARD Programme'. In Niehof, A.; Terpstra, P., ed. *Households in an Interdisciplinary Perspective*. Wageningen University, Wageningen, The Netherlands. pp. 37–46.

CIP-UPWARD. 2006. *Strengthening Regional Capacity for Participatory Research and Development: a Training-based Pilot Project in South Asia* (Project final report). CIP-UPWARD, Los Baños, Laguna, Philippines.

Cooren, F.; Taylor, J.; Van Emery, E.J. 2006. *Communication as Organizing: Empirical and Theoretical Explorations in the Dynamic of Text and Conversation*. Lawrence Erlbaum Associates, Mahwah, New Jersey. pp. 1–16.

COHD (College of Humanities and Development). 2004. 'Participatory Learning, Curriculum Development, and Mainstreaming of CBNRM in Higher Education in China'. Research proposal. China Agricultural University, Beijing, China.

Craig, R. 1999. 'Communication Theory as a Field'. *Communication Theory*, 9(2): 119–161.

Cranton, P. 2006. *Understanding and Promoting Transformative Learning: A Guide for Educators* (2nd ed.). Jossey-Bass, San Francisco, Cal., USA.

Dagli, W. 2006. 'ALL in CBNRM Knowledge Bank: Knowledge Management Strategy in CBNRM'. Presented at the ALL in CBNRM Pilot Introductory Workshop, 19–23 June 2006, College of Development Communication, Laguna, Philippines.

Dao Mong Uyen. 2007. 'Most Significant Changes Related to Participatory Development Communication in Lobster Resource Management in Xuan Dai Bay, Phu Yen Province, Vietnam'. M.Sc. thesis. University of the Philippines, Los Baños, Philippines.

Davies, R.; Dart, J. 2005. *The "Most Significant Change" (MSC) Technique: A Guide to its Use*. MandE, United Kingdom. pp. 104. Available: www.mande.co.uk/docs/MSCGuide.pdf (accessed 27 Oct. 2008).

Dhakal, M.P. 2006. *Building Local Capacity for SRI through PR&D.* In Campilan, D.; Bertuso, A.; Ariyabandu, R.; Sister, L. ed. *Learning Participation in Action: Field Research Experiences in South Asia.* CIP-UPWARD, Los Baños, Laguna, Philippines. pp. 131–141. Available: www.cip-upward.org/main/AMC/snap-ins/DOC/DOC_DocumentsViewer.asp?DocID=1143 (accessed 25 Sept. 2008).

Dhungyel, M.D. and Zangmo. 2006. Understanding Irrigation Transformation for Livelihood Improvement: A Case of Participatory Research and Development in Bhutan'. In Campilan, D.; Bertuso, A.; Ariyabandu, R.; Sister, L. ed. *Learning Participation in Action: Field Research Experiences in South Asia.* CIP-UPWARD, Los Baños, Laguna, Philippines. pp. 31–39. Available: www.cip-upward.org/main/AMC/snapins/DOC/DOC_DocumentsViewer.asp?DocID=1143 (accessed 25 Sept. 2008).

Engel, P.; Keijzer, N.; Land, T. 2007. *A Balanced Approach to Monitoring and Evaluating Capacity and Performance.* European Centre for Development Policy Management, Maastricht, Netherlands. Discussion paper 58E.

Freire, P. 2000. *Pedagogy of the oppressed* (30th anniv. ed.). Continuum, New York, USA, and London, United Kingdom.

Geertz, C. 1977. *The Interpretation of Cultures: Selected Essays.* Basic Books, New York, NY, USA.

Gonsalves, J.; Becker, T.; Braun, A.; Campilan, D.; de Chavez, H.; Fajber, E.; Kapiriri, M.; Rivaca-Caminade, J.; Vernooy, R. ed. 2005. *Participatory Research and Development for Sustainable Agriculture and Natural Resource Management: A Sourcebook.* CIP-UPWARD, Los Baños, Laguna, Philippines, and International Development Research Centre, Ottawa, Canada. 3 Vols. pp. 666.

Habermas, J. 1985. *The Theory of Communicative Action.* Vol. 1: *Reason and the rationalization of society.* Beacon Press, Boston, MA, USA.

Hanson, A.J.; Martin, C. 2006. *One lifeboat: China and the World's Environment and Development.* International Institute for Sustainable Development, Winnipeg, Manitoba, Canada. Available: www.iisd.org/publications/pub.aspx?pno=833 (accessed 17 November 2008).

Horton, D.; Alexaki, A.; Bennett-Lartey, S.; Brice, K.N.; Campilan, D.; Carden, F.; de Souza Silva, J.; Le Than Duong; Kadar, I.; Maestrey Boza, A.; Kayes Muniruzzaman, I; Perez, J.; Somarriba Chang, M.; Vernooy, R.; Watts, J. ed. 2003. *Evaluating Capacity Development: Experiences from Research and Development Organizations Around the World.* ISNAR, The Hague, Netherlands, International Development Research Centre, Ottawa, ON, Canada, and CTA, Leusden, Netherlands. Available: www.idrc.ca/en/ev-31556-201-1-DO_TOPIC.html (accessed 13 Sept. 2008).

Kelly, G.A. 1963. *Theory of Personality: the Psychology of Personal Constructs.* W.W. Norton, New York, NY, USA.

Large, P.J. 2006. 'Towards "centres of excellence" for community Based Natural Resource Management: Exploring Issues of Capacity Development for Organizations and Networks'. Rural Poverty and the Environment Working Paper Series 20. International Development Research Centre, Ottawa, ON, Canada. Available: www.idrc.ca/uploads/user-S/11559183181Patrick_Large_Working_Paper_20.pdf (accessed 13 Sept. 2008).

Leeuwis, C. 2002. Making Explicit the Social Dimension of Cognition. In Leeuwis, C.; Pyburn, R., ed. *Wheelbarrows full of Frogs: Social Learning in Rural Resource Management.* Koninklijke Van Gorcum, Assen, Netherlands. pp. 391–406.

Leeuwis, C.; Pyburn, R., ed. 2002. *Wheelbarrows Full of Frogs: Social Learning in Rural Resource Management.* Koninklijke Van Gorcum, Assen, Netherlands.

Li Xiaoyun; Li Ou. 2003. Learning and Teaching participation in Higher Education in China. *Participatory Learning and Action Notes,* 48: 36–40. Available: www.iied.org/pubs/pdfs/G02065.pdf (accessed 17 November 2008).

Mackay, R.; Horton, D.; Dupleich, L.; Andersen, A. 2002. 'Evaluating Capacity Development'. *Canadian Journal of Programme Evaluation,* 17(2): 121–150.

Mezirow, J. and Associates. 2000. *Learning as Transformation: Critical Perspectives on a Theory in Progress.* Jossey-Bass, San-Francisco, Cal., USA.

Morgan, P. 2006. *The Concept of Capacity.* European Centre for Development Policy Management, Maastricht, Netherlands. Available: www.ecdpm.org/Web_ECDPM/Web/Content/Download.nsf/0/5C9686B6420EC799C12571AF003BCA09/$FILE/Morgan%20-%20Capacity%20-%20What%20is%20it%2010052006.pdf (accessed 13 October 2008).

Nielson, S.; Lusthaus, C. 2007. 'IDRC-supported Capacity Building: Developing a Framework for Capturing Capacity Changes'. International Development Research Centre, Ottawa, ON, Canada. Available: www.idrc.ca/en/ev-111005-201-1-DO_TOPIC.html (accessed 13 Sept. 2008).

Percy, R. 2005. 'The Contribution of Transformative Learning Theory to the Practice of Participatory Research and Extension: Theoretical Reflections.' *Agriculture and Human Values* (22): 127–136.

Pham Tran Thuy Anh. 2007. 'Community-Based Upland Natural Resource Management Researchers' Capacity for Implementation of Participatory Development Communication in Hong Ha Ethnic Commune, A Luoi,

Hue, Vietnam (2002–2004). M.Sc. thesis. University of the Philippines, Los Baños, Philippines.

Qi Gubo; Li Xiaoyun; Zuo Ting; Vernooy, R. 2005. 'Networking for Community-Based Natural Resource Management and Farmer-centred Research: A Case from China'. In Gonsalves, J.; Becker, T.; Braun, A.; Campilan, D.; De Chavez, H.; Fajber, E.; Kapiriri, M.; Rivaca-Caminade, J.; Vernooy, R. ed. *Participatory Research and Development for Sustainable Agriculture and Natural Resource Management: A Sourcebook.* CIP-UPWARD, Los Baños, Philippines and International Development Research Centre, Ottawa, Canada. pp. 104–110.

Qi Gubo; Xu Xiuli; Zuo Ting; Li Xiaoyun; Chen Keke; Gao Xiaowei; Ji Miao; Lin Liu; Mao Miankui; Li Jingsong; Song Yiching; Long Zhipu; Lu Min; Yuan Juanwen; Vernooy, R. 2008. Introducing Participatory Curriculum Development in China's Higher Education: the Case of community-Based Natural Resource Management. *Journal of Agricultural Education and Extension,* 14(1): 7–20.

Röling, N. 2002. 'Beyond the Aggregation of Individual Preferences: Moving from Multiple to Distributed Cognition in Resource Dilemmas'. In Leeuwis, C.; Pyburn, R. ed. *Wheelbarrows Full of Frogs: Social Learning in Rural Resource Management.* Koninklijke Van Gorcum, Assen, Netherlands. pp. 25–47.

Saludadez, J.A. 2004. 'Research Collaboration Stories: Communication as Constitutive of Temporary Organization. Ph.D. Dissertation'. Universiti Putra Malaysia, Selangor, Malaysia.

Sharma, K.K.; Pathak, P.K. 2006. 'Cultural Diversity in Selection of Upland "Ahu" Rice Varieties in Southern Part of Brahmaputra River'. In Campilan, D.; Bertuso, A.; Ariyabandu, R.; Sister, L. (editor) *Learning Participation in Action: Field Research Experiences in South Asia.* CIP-UPWARD, Los Baños, Laguna, Philippines. pp. 95–104. Available: www.cip-upward.org/main/AMC/snap-ins/DOC/DOC_DocumentsViewer.asp?DocID=1143 (accessed 25 Sept. 2008).

Sreedevi, T.K. 2006. 'Capitalizing on Powerguda's Capitals to Improve Livelihoods'. In Campilan, D.; Bertuso, A.; Ariyabandu, R.; Sister, L. ed. *Learning Participation in Action: Field Research Experiences in South Asia.* CIP-UPWARD, Los Baños, Laguna, Philippines. pp. 19–29. Available: www.cip-upward.org/main/AMC/snapins/DOC/DOC_DocumentsViewer.asp?DocID=1143 (accessed 25 Sept. 2008).

Song Yiching; Zhang Linxiu; Vernooy, R. 2006. 'Empowering Women Farmers and Strengthening the Local Seed System: Action Research in Guangxi, China'. In Vernooy, R. ed. *Integrating Social and Gender Analysis in Natural Resource Management: Learning Studies and Lessons from Asia.* Sage, New Delhi, India, International Development Research Centre, Ottawa, Canada, and China Agricultural Press, Beijing, China. pp. 99–128.

Taylor, P. 2003. *How to Design a Training Course: Participatory Curriculum Development.* Volunteer Services Overseas, London, UK.

Taylor, P.; Fransman, J. 2004. *Learning and Teaching Participation: Exploring the Role of Higher Learning Institutions as Agents of Development and Social Change.* Institute of Development Studies, Brighton, UK. IDS working paper 219.

Tirol, S.C.; Abraham, E.; Rodantes G.; Torres, C.S.; Flor, B.P.G.; Matulac, L.A.; Domingo, I.V.D.; Dagli, W.B. 2007. 'Evaluating Capacity Development in the Adaptive Learning and Linkages in Community-Based Natural Resource Management Programme. Unpublished proposal. CIP-UPWARD, Los Baños, Laguna, Philippines.

Tyler S.R. ed. 2006. *Communities, Livelihoods and Natural Resources: Action Research and Policy Change in Asia.* Intermediate Technology Publications, Bourton on Dunsmore, United Kingdom, and International Development Research Centre, Ottawa, Canada.

Van den Bor, W.; Holen, P.; Wals, A.; Leal Filho, W. ed. 2000. *Integrating Concepts of Sustainability into Education for Agriculture and Rural Development.* Peter Lang, Frankfurt am Main, Germany.

Vernooy, R. 2003. *In focus: Seeds that Give – Participatory Plant Breeding.* International Development Research Centre, Ottawa, Canada. Available: www.idrc.ca/en/ev-30294-201-1-DO_TOPIC.html (accessed 11 Dec. 2008).

Vernooy, R. ed. 2006. *Integrating Social and Gender Analysis in Natural Resource Management: Learning Studies and Lessons from Asia.* Sage, New Delhi, India, International Development Research Centre, Ottawa, Canada, and China Agricultural Press, Beijing, China.

Vernooy, R.; Hijaba, Y.; Enkhbat, B.; Ulipkan, B.; Graham, J. 2005. 'Challenges of Participatory Natural Resource Management Research'. In Gonsalves, J.; Becker, T.; Braun, A.; Campilan, D.; De Chavez, H.; Fajber, E.; Kapiriri, M.; Rivaca-Caminade, J.; Vernooy, R. ed. *Participatory Research and Development for Sustainable Agriculture and Natural Resource Management: A Sourcebook.* CIP-UPWARD, Los Baños, Philippines, and International Development Research Centre, Ottawa, Canada. pp. 220–227.

Vernooy, R.; Li Xiaoyun; Xu Xiuli; Lu Min; Qi Gubo. ed. 2008. *Learning from the Field: Innovating China's Higher Education System.* Cambridge University Press, New Delhi, India, and International Development Research Centre, Ottawa, Canada.

Vernooy, R.; Yiching Song. 2004. 'New Approaches to Supporting the Agricultural Biodiversity Important for Sustainable Rural Livelihoods'. *International Journal of Agricultural Sustainability,* 2(1): 55–66.

Vernooy, R.; Sun Qiu; Xu Jianchu. ed. 2003. *Voices for Change: Participatory Monitoring and Evaluation in China.* Yunnan Science and Technology

Press, Kunming, China, and International Development Research Centre, Ottawa, Canada.

Vernooy, R.; Sun Qiu; Xu Jianchu. 2006. *The Power of Participatory Monitoring and Evaluation: Insights from South-West China. Development in Practice* 16(5): 400-411.

Wals, A.J. ed. 2007. *Social Learning for Sustainability.* Wageningen University Press, Wageningen, Netherlands.

Watson, D. 2006. *Monitoring and Evaluation of Capacity and Capacity Development.* Discussion paper 58B. European Centre for Development Policy Management, Maastricht, The Netherlands: 32 pp. Available: www.ecdpm.org/dp58B (accessed 13 October 2008).

Wenger, E. 1998. *Communities of Practice: Learning, Meaning and Identity.* Cambridge University Press, Cambridge, United Kingdom.

Wenger, E.; McDermott, R.; Snyder, W.M. 2002. *Cultivating Communities of Practice: A Guide to Managing Knowledge.* Harvard Business School, Boston, Mass, USA.

Weragoda, R. L. and Hettige, S.N. 2006. 'Coping with Vulnerabilities: Participatory Assessment of Vulnerabilities of Coastal Communities for Sustainable Livelihood and Natural Resource Management'. In Campilan, D.; Bertuso, A.; Ariyabandu, R.; Sister, L. ed. *Learning Participation in Action: Field Research Rxperiences in South Asia.* CIP-UPWARD, Los Baños, Laguna, Philippines. pp. 9–18. Available: www.cip-upward.org/main/AMC/snap-ins/DOC/DOC_DocumentsViewer.asp?DocID=1143 (accessed 25 Sept. 2008).

Yin, R.K. 2008. *Case Study Research: Design and Methods.* Sage Publishing, Thousands Oaks, Cal., USA.

Yuan Juanwen; Sun Qiu. 2006. 'Scaling up Community-Based Natural Resource Management in Guizhou Province, China'. In Tyler, S.R. ed. *Communities, Livelihoods and Natural Resources: Action Research and Policy Change in Asia.* Intermediate Technology Publications, Bourton on Dunsmore, United Kingdom, and International Development Research Centre, Ottawa, Canada. pp. 169–190. Available: www.idrc.ca/en/ev-103648-201-1-DO_TOPIC.html (accessed 17 November 2008).

Zhang Li. 2008. *Into a New Orbit: changing China's Higher Education System, in Person.* China Agricultural University Press, Beijing, China.

Zhou Ji. 2006. *Higher education in China.* Thomson, Singapore.

Notes on Contributors

Rajindra Ariyabandu is Development Researcher with a special interest in water resources management and community development. He has an experience of twenty years of working in various capacities with government and nongovernmental organizations and international research institutions. He has been actively involved in water policy development and coordination of regional water resources management for the last ten years. He has extensive field research experience in the implementation of low-cost, community-managed water utilities for rural poor. Rajindra is currently involved in compiling a "reader" on community water governance in South Asia.

Carlos Basilio is Food Security Specialist at Christian Children's Fund in Timor Leste. Until 2006, he was a research fellow with Centro Internacional de la Papa's Users' Perspectives with Agricultural Research and Development in the Philippines (CIP-UPWARD), where he was responsible for participatory research on integrated crop management and training support for participatory research and development. Earlier, he was the Philippines' country programme coordinator for the Center for Information on Low External Input and Sustainable Agriculture. He has a Ph.D. in environmental science from the University of the Philippines Los Baños.

Guy Bessette is Senior Programme Specialist at the International Development Research Centre in Ottawa. His work focuses on participatory development communication, social learning, and participatory research for community-based natural resource management (CBNRM). He has a Ph.D. in education from the University of Montreal, Canada.

Maria Celeste H. Cadiz is Training and Knowledge Manager at the Southeast Asian Regional Center for Graduate Study and Research in Agriculture in the Philippines. She is also an associate professor and was the first dean of the College of Development Communication of the University of the Philippines Los Baños (UPLB). She has devoted her thirty-year career to teaching, research, and practice in development communication, with a focus on educational communication, participatory communication, interpersonal communication in development, and communication research and theory. She holds a Ph.D. from Macquarie University in New South Wales, Australia, and a degree in development communication (*cum laude*) from UPLB.

Dindo Campilan is Social Scientist at the Centro Internacional de la Papa and leader of UPWARD, CIP's Asia-wide network for participatory research and development. His work covers participatory research, capacity development and partnerships, monitoring and evaluation, and markets and value chains. Since June 2008, he has been serving as CIP's regional leader for South, West and Central Asia and is based in New Delhi, India. He has a Ph.D. in communication and innovation studies from Wageningen University, The Netherlands.

Winifredo B. Dagli is Knowledge Management Associate at the Earthquakes and Megacities Initiative and was Project Officer of the Adaptive Learning and Linkages in Community-Based Natural Resource Management (ALL in CBNRM) programme. His work focuses on research and writing for various development projects on disaster and risk management, CBNRM, environmental conservation, biotechnology, food security, gender, and knowledge management. He is currently preparing his master's thesis on the political ecology of national protected areas under the sociology programme of the University of the Philippines Diliman. He has a bachelor's degree in development communication (*cum laude)* specializing in science communication from the same university, Los Baños campus.

Julian Gonsalves is a Freelance Development Consultant and currently Senior Adviser to CIP-UPWARD. Previously, he was vice-president, programme, at the International Institute of Rural Reconstruction in the Philippines. His areas of professional interest and expertise include pro-poor agriculture research and natural resource management, research partnerships and networking, sustainable agriculture, participatory monitoring and evaluation, and farmer-led extension. He has a Ph.D. in extension and international agriculture from Cornell University in the United States.

Jingsong Li has a B.Sc. degree in sociology from China Agricultural University, Beijing, and a master's degree in environmental management from Wageningen Agricultural University in the Netherlands. She works as a Senior Research Assistant at the Centre for Chinese Agricultural Policy and has a special interest in rural development and environmental management. She is currently pursuing Ph.D. studies on conservation of genetic resources, traditional knowledge, and farmers' rights at Wageningen University.

Kevin Kelpin was a member of IDRC's Evaluation Unit from 2002 to 2007. He currently lives in India and works with organizations in South Asia, Southeast Asia and Africa, enhancing their skills in monitoring and evaluation, strategic planning, and knowledge management.

Long Zhipu is Head of Ningxia for Environmental Protection and Poverty Alleviation (HOPE). He graduated from the Agriculture College of Ningxia University in 1984 with specializations in agriculture, animal extension work, and desertification control. Since 1997, he has participated in a number of internationally supported projects with a focus on agricultural development, poverty reduction, women's development, micro-credit, and CBNRM.

Raghav Raj Regmi is Development Consultant operating in Nepal and South Asia, who has worked with Verulam Associates since 2000. His areas of professional expertise and interest include training in participatory rural appraisal and participatory action research in the agriculture, education, and health sectors; NGO–project management; organizational development; and capacity building. He has a master's degree in development management from the Asian Institute of Management in the Philippines.

Pratap Shrestha is Senior Advisor of Local Initiatives for Biodiversity, Research and Development in Nepal. His areas of professional interest and expertise include participatory crop improvement, sustainable agricultural livelihoods, participatory technology development, CBNRM, NGO management, participatory training, and farmer-led extension. He has a Ph.D. in natural resource management from the University of Wales, Bangor, United Kingdom. Previously, he was a senior researcher at the Lumle Agricultural Research Centre.

Qi Gubo is a graduate of the College of Economics and Management at Beijing Agricultural University. After obtaining her Ph.D. degree, she joined the staff of the College of Economics and Management. She is now at the College of Humanities and Development (COHD), China Agricultural University, Beijing, where she is a full time Professor, Rural Development Researcher, and Director of the Rural

Development and Management Programme. Since 2005, she has been leading the working groups, responsible for the CBNRM course for Master's and Doctorate students.

Ronnie Vernooy is Senior Programme Specialist at the International Development Research Centre, Ottawa, Canada. He received his Ph.D. in the sociology of rural development from Wageningen Agricultural University, the Netherlands. He has conducted and directed a number of rural development research projects in Nicaragua and currently contributes actively to CBNRM research efforts in a number of countries in Asia including China, Viet Nam, and Mongolia. Since 2005, he has also been an adjunct professor at COHD.

Zhang Li obtained her Master of Science degree in Regional Economics from China Agricultural University in 2005 and her Ph.D. in Rural Development and Management from the same university in 2009. She was a student assistant for the 2006 CBNRM course and a co-facilitator for the 2007 course at COHD. In 2008, she was a research intern with the Rural Poverty and Environment Programme of the International Development Research Centre in Ottawa, Canada. She is now a research fellow at the Development Research Centre of the China Association for Science and Technology, Beijing.

Index